Common Core State Standards for Grades K–1

Language Arts Instructional Strategies and Activities

Michelle Manville

ROWMAN & LITTLEFIELD EDUCATION
A division of
ROWMAN & LITTLEFIELD
Lanham • Boulder • New York • Toronto • Plymouth, UK

Published by Rowman & Littlefield Education
A division of Rowman & Littlefield
4501 Forbes Boulevard, Suite 200, Lanham, Maryland 20706
www.rowman.com

10 Thornbury Road, Plymouth PL6 7PP, United Kingdom

British Library Cataloguing in Publication Information Available

Library of Congress Cataloging-in-Publication Data

Manville, Michelle, 1953–
Common core state standards for grades K–1 : language arts instructional strategies and activities / Michelle Manville.
  pages cm
Includes bibliographical references.
ISBN 978-1-4758-0663-2 (pbk. : alk. paper)—ISBN 978-1-4758-0664-9 (electronic)
1. Language arts—Standards—United States. 2. Education, Elementary—Activity programs—United States. 3. Early childhood education—Activity programs—United States. I. Title.
LB1576.M37756 2013
372.6—dc23
2013021143

Printed in the United States of America

Contents

Contents

Introduction

The Common Core State Standards (CCSS) for English Language Arts and Literacy in History/Social Studies, Science, and Technical Subjects were developed to ensure that students are ready for the challenges of college and career literacy by the end of their high school years. The Standards were developed around K–12 grade-specific areas of reading literature and informational text, writing, speaking and listening, and language. These research- and evidence-based Standards are rigorous and are aligned to the College and Career Readiness anchor standards, which establish what all students should know and be able to do upon entering post-secondary institutions.

At a time when schools across the nation are looking for ways to improve student achievement in most content areas, it seems reasonable to combine the standards and effective instructional strategies as you create activities to help with the implementation of the CCSS.

When you look at the CCSS, think of the standards as representative of what students need to know and be able to do and what you need to do as a teacher to help them be successful. Based on the identified CCSS and other skills, students need to know how to compare and contrast; summarize information and take notes; create visual representations of information; work together collaboratively; conduct research; and be able to ask and answer higher-order questions. Additionally to help students achieve success, teachers need to provide ample opportunities to practice new skills and demonstrate and enhance new learning.

A multitude of studies have been conducted over the past thirty years. From these studies, Education Northwest, formerly Northwest Regional Education Laboratory (2005), compiled a list of effective instructional strategies with descriptions, research findings, and implementation suggestions. When developing activities to address CCSS, keep in mind the strategies of identifying similarities and differences, summarizing, non-linguistic representations, cooperative learning, generating and testing hypotheses, questions, cues, advanced organizers, and homework and practice. As teachers, provide many opportunities for homework and practice as you implement the Common Core State Standards.

There's no guarantee that activities based on any strategy will help in every instance, and it may be quite possible that some strategies are more effective in certain subject areas and grade levels and with students from different backgrounds and aptitudes. Whether or not you use a strategy will depend on your students' previous knowledge and current abilities.

It is the intent of this book to give teachers a ready-made resource to use when planning lessons around Common Core State Standards. In each section you will find grade-appropriate, ready-to-use activities aligned to specific Common Core State Standards in English Language Arts and Literacy in History/Social Studies, Science, and Technical Subjects. All you need to supply is the content-rich text.

It is my hope that you will find this an essential component of your instructional materials as you plan your curriculum for the students of the twenty-first century.

ONE

Instructional Strategies and Activities: An Overview

Many of the Common Core State Standards can be taught and reinforced using a variety of activities combined with CCSS and effective instructional strategies. According to Visual Teaching Alliance (www.visualteachingalliance.com), "approximately 65 percent of the population are visual learners" and "90 percent of the information that comes to the brain is visual." The VTA also states that "the brain processes visual information 60,000 times faster than text" and that "visual aids in the classroom improve learning by up to 400 percent."

The use of graphic organizers—visuals—enables students to better organize their thinking and gives a visual frame of reference for information. Students are able to see the connections between previous learning and new knowledge. Graphic organizers increase students' abilities to use higher-order thinking skills, facilitate retention of information, are very brain-friendly, and appeal to the multiple intelligences of visual-spatial, verbal-linguistic, logical-mathematical, and naturalist. The use of graphic organizers also helps those students who are ESL or ELL learners comprehend concepts more easily as there are fewer words to comprehend.

When you write lesson plans, think about the various graphic organizers you can use in activities: T-charts, Venn diagrams, matrices, concept maps, word webs, mind maps, graphs, chains, flowcharts, and lists. Several suggestions are given throughout this book, but you may find a different organizer to help you help your students link new information to old or organize thoughts. Not all organizers are age or grade appropriate so choose carefully.

For those Standards that are not appropriate for graphic organizers, you will find suggestions for a wide variety of structures that you can use

1

in your classrooms. The ideas you find do not represent a definitive list and you may adapt those suggestions to use in other instances.

The instructional strategies described on the next few pages have been identified as effective practices by various educational practitioners based on a multitude of research. *Common Core State Standards for Grades K–1: Language Arts Instructional Strategies and Activities* addresses the use of these strategies with respect to the K–12 Common Core State Standards for English Language Arts and Literacy in History/Social Studies, Science, and Technical Subjects and provides a multitude of ready-to-use activities.

SIMILARITIES AND DIFFERENCES

When students identify similarities and differences, the process helps students deepen the understanding of what they are learning. According to Markman and Gentner (1996), identifying similarities and differences is a basic cognitive process. Students use the processes of comparing, classifying, creating metaphors, and creating analogies to describe how items, events, processes, or concepts are similar or different.

Comparison and/or contrast activities help students to better comprehend new concepts and allows the connection of new knowledge to existing concepts. Teachers should not only point out similarities and differences to students, but should also allow students to develop their own strategies for comparing similarities and differences (http://netc.org/focus/strategies/iden.php).

K–1 Activities

Activities to identify similarities and differences at K–1 include teacher facilitated T-charts, 2-circle Venn diagrams, classification charts, lists, graphs, maps, analogies, 5W and How charts, time lines, mind maps, or word webs.

SUMMARIZING

Summarizing occurs unconsciously for most of us, and children at the K–1 grade level will want to tell you everything they know, whether it is related to the subject or not. We need to teach students to give us only the important details—eliminating the trivialities not necessary for comprehension. Valerie Anderson and Suzanne Hidi synthesized various studies on summarization. According to Anderson and Hidi (1998/1999), when you first begin teaching summarization, be sure to choose short excerpts with easy text, such as narratives or texts with familiar concepts and ideas. Anderson and Hidi (1998/1999) also indicate that students need to be able to select or delete what is included and then reduce the information into a manageable amount.

Kindergarten Summarization

Kindergarten students can begin to give details about events, though will not necessarily give the key details. Teachers can model summarization skills and can guide Kindergarten students through the steps of summarization using various activities.

Kindergarten Activities

Common summarization activities for Kindergarten include the use of teacher-facilitated time lines, webs, and 5W and How charts. Teachers can write the graphic organizers on chart paper or on the board and can fill in the details in class or group discussion. Other activities include drawing pictures and role-playing important actions and events.

Grade 1 Summarization

Students in Grade 1 can begin to use teacher-facilitated summary frames to help develop summarization skills. The use of summary frames helps students select and reduce information for summaries using specific questions and helps students develop a deeper comprehension of the information read. A summary frame is an effective structure when summarizing reading assignments. Studies by Meyer and Freedle (1984) show that reading comprehension increases when students learn how to incorporate summary frames. Summary frames also help students to focus on important information and allow teachers to determine the depth of comprehension through student responses.

Types of Summary Frames

Narrative or story frames include information about the characters, setting, actions, feelings, and goals of the main character, and the consequences.

Definition frames use four questions: What concept is being defined? To which category does the item belong? What are the attributes or characteristics of the concept? What examples are given to illustrate the concept?

Grade 1 Activities

Common summarization activities for Grade 1 include the use of teacher-facilitated narrative, or story, and definition summary frames, modified acrostics, time lines, webs, and 5W and How charts. Teachers can post or draw the forms on chart paper or on the board and can fill in the details in class or group discussion. See Appendix B for examples of summary frames.

TAKING NOTES

Grade 1 students do not necessarily "take notes." They can, however, begin to grasp the concept of taking notes by watching the teacher jot down on chart paper or the board key ideas or words or phrases to remember about a topic. Teachers can use graphic organizers, outlines, mnemonic devices, Alphaboxes, concept maps, T-charts, and Venn diagrams to begin to teach students to write down key points. Other activities include reading outside or in a special place in the classroom; using content-related visuals (such as posters, charts, and representative artifacts) in the classroom; and listening to background music or creating songs or pictures that represent key concepts. See Appendix A for an example of an Alphabox.

NONLINGUISTIC REPRESENTATIONS

When students use nonlinguistic representations in activities, they use movement, some words, pictures, and symbols to convey knowledge while learning. The use of this strategy helps students synthesize information in a way that makes sense to them and are then better able to retain and recall the information. In most classroom applications, students and teachers will combine words in graphic organizers with the nonlinguistic representations. The use of visual representations helps students recognize how concepts are connected (NCTM, 2000).

There are many examples of mind maps, or webs, or pictorial representations you can use in the classroom. You will undoubtedly have to teach students how to create these representations. Spencer Kagan (1998a) offers these helpful hints when creating mind maps including: "use white space, practice symbols and images, emphasize important images, and practice." Students can also create pictographs that use representative pictures or symbols to present information.

The brain is a pattern-seeking device; nonlinguistic representations are patterns. Use of these patterns can help nearly all students, especially the visual-spatial student, comprehend and retain information. The use of patterns helps students organize their thinking and helps them apply what they have learned (Bransford et al., 1999; Lehrer & Chazen, 1998).

Nonlinguistic representation activities create visuals, and according to Lehrer and Chazen (1998), "by ignoring visualization, curricula not only fail to engage a powerful part of students' minds in service of their mathematical thinking, but also fail to develop students' skills at visual exploration and argument" (p. 6). The ability to visualize can also serve the language arts student as well.

K–1 Activities

To create activities for Kindergarten–Grade 1 nonlinguistic representations, include role-playing and dramatizations; kinesthetic activities such as marching, clapping or dancing, or writing in sand, finger paint, or with clay; recordings of favorite passages or stories; oral readings, narrations, and recitations; listening to recordings; creating physical models with macaroni or sugar cubes; and drawings and creating other pictorial representations such as collages, murals, pictographs, or posters.

COOPERATIVE LEARNING

A graphic attributed to American psychiatrist William Glasser, based on a graphic created by Edgar Dale (1969, p. 108), indicates: We learn 10 percent of what we read, 20 percent of what we hear, 30 percent of what we see, 50 percent of what we see and hear, 70 percent of what we discuss with others, 80 percent of what we experience, and 95 percent of what we teach to others. Perhaps an easier way to describe Glasser's view of learning is "two heads are better than one."

What Is Cooperative Learning?

Cooperative learning is *not* group work. It *is* where two or more students work together cooperatively to achieve a common goal. According to Johnson and Johnson (1999) (as cited in Education Northwest, formerly Northwest Regional Educational Laboratory, 2005, para. 1) "effective cooperative learning occurs when students work together to accomplish shared goals and when positive structures are in place to support that process." Students in Kindergarten–Grade 1 should continue to work with others as the concept of cooperative learning is a lifelong lesson that will help them throughout their lives.

Teachers and students alike are often placed into group settings where either everyone or no one is in charge; where chaos reigns; where nothing is accomplished. Unless you know how to work in a group, the group is almost certainly doomed. When groups work within specific guidelines, there will be more student interaction, inquiry thinking, time-on-task, in-depth questions, and student accountability. Shy students will feel safe. Studies show that cooperative learning enhances student performance and should not be based on competition.

A Teacher's Role in Cooperative Learning

The teacher's role in cooperative learning includes selecting the group size, assignment of students to the groups, arranging the classroom, providing appropriate materials, setting the task and goal structure, monitoring student-student interaction, intervening to solve problems and teach skills, and evaluating the outcome(s) (Johnson & Johnson, 1999).

Sometimes teachers will want to assign specific roles to specific students or you may want to give a list of possible roles to students and let them work it out. You will always want to make sure that roles rotate among the students. The number of roles you have will obviously depend on the number of students in a group and the nature of the work to be done in the group. You might want to create roles such as: leader, recorder or secretary, checker, speaker, facilitator, timekeeper, summarizer, and reflector (http://serc.carleton.edu/introgeo/cooperative/roles.html).

K–1 Activities

Cooperative learning activities for Kindergarten–Grade 1 include the Kagan Cooperative Learning structures (Kagan & Kagan, 1997) of Find My Rule, Snowball, and Team-Pair-Solo. Other activities include peer editing and revising, conducting research, publishing, collaborative discussions, and group presentations.

GENERATING AND TESTING HYPOTHESES

Students must learn to question in order to question to learn. Students who are able to generate and test their hypotheses—ask questions and explain their hypotheses—will greatly enhance their own learning. Children begin to ask questions as soon as they begin talking and continue to ask questions through adulthood. Teachers can help students learn to ask good questions that will help them make better hypotheses. Students who are able to explain their hypotheses will demonstrate their understanding of concepts as well.

Research Findings

According to Lavoie and Good (1998) and Lawson (1998) (as cited in Education Northwest, formerly Northwest Regional Educational Laboratory, 2005, para. 3) "understanding increases when students are asked to explain the scientific principles they are working from and the hypotheses they generate from these principles."

Similarly, White and Frederickson (1998) (as cited in Education Northwest, formerly Northwest Regional Educational Laboratory, 2005, para.

5) found that when comparing "inquiry-based instruction and traditional teaching methods (such as lectures and textbook-based instruction), researchers found that inquiry methods helped students gain a better understanding of fundamental science concepts." These ideas can be applied to language arts, too.

Applications for Language Arts Classrooms

The ability to generate and test hypotheses isn't just for science anymore. For example, a language arts teacher could ask students to read literature, predict the actions of one or more of the characters, and then read and discuss the accuracy of the predictions (Kuhn, 2009). Leach (2010) describes how teachers show students various pictures dealing with short stories or novels they are reading and how teachers ask students to predict the outcome of events based on the pictures. Students can also predict the ending of a story at the middle of a story or book and discuss the accuracy of their hypotheses at the end.

Seize the opportunity to use the natural curiosity of all students. They love to question why we do things, so turn it around on them and let them discover why and what. Teach students the art of asking strong, higher-order questions, and challenge them to explain the results of their findings.

K–1 Activities

Classroom activities for Kindergarten–Grade 1 generating and testing hypotheses include facilitating students in creating and testing hypotheses, making predictions, solving problems, conducting historical investigations, making observations, and making decisions based on information. See Appendix C for a list of stem questions and Appendix H for a list of higher- and lower-order questions.

CUES, QUESTIONS, AND ADVANCE ORGANIZERS

The brain, as a pattern-seeking device, looks to link new information to previous knowledge. When we use cues, questions, and advance organizers, we access what students already know and prepare them for what they are about to learn.

Research Findings

Marzano et al. (2001) found (as cited in Davis & Tinsley, 1967; Fillippone, 1998) that "cueing and questioning might account for as much as 80 percent of what occurs in a given classroom on a given day" (p. 113). If we are asking that many questions, then we need to consider the quality of the questions we ask. Are we asking questions that reflect the most important content? Do we ask higher-order questions or do we simply ask students to recall information?

Redfield and Rousseau (1981) found that asking higher-level questions, rather than asking recall questions, requires students to analyze information which results in more learning. Do teachers tend to ask more lower-order questions? Do we use questions, cues, and advance organizers to focus learning? Are we waiting long enough for students to give more thoughtful responses? Do we give some students longer to respond because of who they are? T. W. Fowler (1975) found that when teachers are taught a technique related to the amount of wait time after asking a question, students are more likely to participate and participate more frequently in small group student-to-student interactions.

Determine the Types of Questions Asked

One way to determine the types of questions you use in the classroom is to audiotape several instructional sessions in your classroom. This will give you the opportunity to hear how much wait time you give and to whom. Using the "Verbs to Question" in Appendix H, mark the verbs you use in your class. If you use more lower-order verbs in instruction, then use more higher-order verbs. If you teach more than one content area, you might want to tape instruction in various content areas and see what types of questions you ask. Maybe there is a correlation to the content area where you ask the higher- or lower-order questions.

You can also create a list of higher-order, grade-appropriate verbs and post them in your classroom. You may wish to choose verbs from Appendix H. When you use K-W-L charts, use the list to help improve the questions on your chart. If we do not use higher-order questions in our classroom instruction, then we cannot expect students to ask them either.

Use Cues and Questions

Cues are hints or reminders that help access prior knowledge and are generally explicit in nature. In the book *Checking for Understanding: Formative Assessment Techniques for Your Classroom*, Douglas Fisher and Nancy Frey (2007) suggest teachers use symbols, words, or phrases to help students recall information. Fisher and Frey (2007) also suggest using direct eye contact, facial expressions, body posture, physical distance, silence, short verbal acknowledgments, and sub-summaries (restating or paraphrasing main ideas).

Questions can act as cues or require students to analyze information. Questions should engage students in their learning and increase participation in the classroom. Fisher and Frey (2007) identified several strategies that are helpful in questioning. These strategies include response cards, hand signals, and audience response systems.

Advance Organizers

Sometimes you need more than a cue or question. Use advance organizers when introducing new concepts as they will help link previous knowledge to the new learning that is going to take place. Advance organizers are organizational frameworks that provide guidance as to the important information in a lesson or unit. Information that is presented graphically and symbolically reinforces reading and learning skills (Brookbank, Grover, Kullberg, & Strawser, 1999).

K–1 Activities

When creating activities around questions, cues, and advance organizers for Kindergarten–Grade 1 include the use of higher-order questions, using visual cues and advance organizers such as narrative frames, time lines, and webs. See Appendix D for sample Kindergarten Advance Organizers and Appendix E for sample Grade 1 Advance Organizers.

HOMEWORK AND PRACTICE

Thomas Edison once said that "genius is 2 percent inspiration and 98 percent perspiration" and he felt that hard work would get one to the "top rung of Fortune's ladder" (Jones 1908, p. 347). It is up to us to make homework and practice meaningful to students so that their 98 percent perspiration will help them become the geniuses they can be. Create a variety of activities that enable students to practice the CCSS skills.

Homework activities should not be busy work. The activities should have a purpose that is clearly articulated to students. In the book, *Rethinking Homework: Best Practices That Support Diverse Needs*, Cathy Vatterott (2009) suggests homework be given to help the learning process in four ways: pre-learning, checking for understanding, practice, and processing. It is important to prepare students for new content and for teachers to find out what students already know about the content. K-W-L chart activities are good to use for teacher-facilitated pre-learning. Vatterott (2009) also states that checking for understanding "is the most neglected use of homework, yet it is the most valuable way for teachers to gain insight into student learning" (p. 97).

There is an old adage that says "practice makes perfect." However, many believe practice makes better and that only perfect practice makes perfect. The very essence of homework is to provide such practice, especially for rote skills—saying the alphabet, counting, and naming the months of the year. But if students do not understand a concept and teachers do not check for understanding, then the practice could lead to misconceptions and inaccurate learning.

Suggestions for Parents

Kindergarten can be a beginning grade level for homework and practice. Talk with your parents at back-to-school night or at Kindergarten Round-Up about homework and practice expectations in your classroom. Share the purposes of homework as those of reinforcing information learned at school, establishing a routine, and developing good study habits. Encourage parents to be involved by sitting with the child as he or she works. Appropriate activities would include repetition and simple skills, such as coloring pictures, counting out loud, or writing letters of the alphabet.

Research Findings and Recommendations

According to Harris Cooper (1989) "it is better to distribute material across several assignments rather than have homework concentrate only on material covered in class that day" (p. 89). Students need to process new information as they link it to previous knowledge. Processing is where students reflect on concepts by considering specific questions to ask, applying information learned, and making connections to a bigger picture (Vatterott, 2009).

In conversations with parents about homework and practice, also let parents know about the frequency of assignments. Some teachers send home "assignments" on Monday to be completed and returned on Friday; others may use Friday to Friday schedules. This allows the student time to process and link new information learned. Choose a schedule that best suits your students and your time constraints.

K–1 Activities

Kindergarten–Grade 1 homework and practice activities include reading and writing practices, word and phrase flashcards, word lists, time lines, and classification charts. See Appendix F for a sample parent letter.

LET'S GET STARTED!

Now you have an overview of various instructional strategies and activities to use with the Common Core State Standards. The rest of the book is devoted to specific activities to use with the strands of reading literature, reading informational text, reading foundational skills, writing, speaking and listening, and language. Within each strand you will find many ready-to-use grade level appropriate activities aligned to specific standards. Many activities will incorporate other standards as well.

You will also find a list of the grade level text exemplars; you are not expected to use the exemplars, but if you have them in your classroom, use them. There are many other wonderful, grade appropriate books listed for you and your students to use if the exemplars are not available to you. Other selections are suggested within the activities.

I hope you find this a valuable tool as you implement the CCSS in your classroom.

TWO
Grades K–1 Text Exemplars

STORIES

Arnold, Tedd. *Hi! Fly Guy*
DePaola, Tomie. *Pancakes for Breakfast*
Eastman, P. D. *Are You My Mother?*
Lobel, Arnold. *Frog and Toad Together*
Lobel, Arnold. *Owl at Home*
Lopshire, Robert. *Put Me in the Zoo*
Minarik, Else Holmelund. *Little Bear*
Seuss, Dr. *Green Eggs and Ham*

POETRY

Agee, Jon. "Two Tree Toads"
Anonymous. "As I Was Going to St. Ives"
Chute, Marchette. "Drinking Fountain"
Ciardi, John. "Wouldn't You?"
Fyleman, Rose. "Singing-Time"
Giovanni, Nikki. "Covers"
Greenfield, Eloise. "By Myself"
Hughes, Langston. "Poem"
Lopez, Alonzo. "Celebration"
Merriam, Eve. "It Fell in the City"
Milne, A. A. "Halfway Down"
Rossetti, Christina. "Mix a Pancake"
Wright, Richard. "Laughing Boy"

READ-ALOUD STORIES

Atwater, Richard and Florence. *Mr. Popper's Penguins*
Bang, Molly. *The Paper Crane*
Baum, L. Frank. *The Wonderful Wizard of Oz*
Garza, Carmen Lomas. *Family Pictures*
Haley, Gail E. *A Story, a Story*
Henkes, Kevin. *Kitten's First Full Moon*
Jansson, Tove. *Finn Family Moomintroll*
Mora, Pat. *Tomas and the Library Lady*
Wilder, Laura Ingalls. *Little House in the Big Woods*
Young, Ed. *Lon Po Po: A Red-Riding Hood Story from China*

READ-ALOUD POETRY

Anonymous. "The Fox's Foray"
Hughes, Langston. "April Rain Song"
Langstaff, John. "Over in the Meadow"
Lear, Edward. "The Owl and the Pussycat"
Moss, Lloyd. "Zin! Zin! Zin! A Violin"

INFORMATIONAL TEXTS

Aliki. *A Weed Is a Flower: The Life of George Washington Carver*
Aliki. *My Five Senses*
Bulla, Clyde Robert. *A Tree Is a Plant*
Crews, Donald. *Truck*
"Garden Helpers." *National Geographic Young Explorers*
Hoban, Tana. *I Read Signs*
Hurd, Edith Thacher. *Starfish*
Reid, Mary Ebeltoft. *Let's Find Out about Ice Cream*
"Wind Power." *National Geographic Young Explorers*

READ-ALOUD INFORMATIONAL TEXTS

Dorros, Arthur. *Follow the Water from Brook to Ocean*
Gibbons, Gail. *Fire! Fire!*
Hodgkins, Fran, and True Kelley. *How People Learned to Fly*
Jenkins, Steve, and Robin Page. *What Do You Do with a Tail Like This?*

Llewellyn, Claire. *Earthworms*
Pfeffer, Wendy. *From Seed to Pumpkin*
Provensen, Alice and Martin. *The Year at Maple Hill Farm*
Rauzon, Mark, and Cynthia Overbeck Bix. *Water, Water Everywhere*
Thomson, Sarah L. *Amazing Whales!*

NOTE

A complete list of text exemplars, standards, and resource materials as identified by the National Governors Association Center for Best Practices can be found at http://corestandards.org/ELA-Literacy.

THREE

Kindergarten Common Core State Standards

READING LITERATURE

RL.K.1—With prompting and support, ask and answer questions about key details in a text.

RL.K.2—With prompting and support, retell familiar stories, including key details.

RL.K.3—With prompting and support, identify characters, settings, and major events in a story.

RL.K.4—Ask and answer questions about unknown words in a text.

RL.K.5—Recognize common types of texts (e.g., storybooks, poems).

RL.K.6—With prompting and support, name the author and illustrator of a story and define the role of each in telling the story.

RL.K.7—With prompting and support, describe the relationship between illustrations and the story in which they appear (e.g., what moment in a story an illustrator depicts).

RL.K.9—With prompting and support, compare and contrast the adventures and experiences of characters in familiar stories.

RL.K.10—Actively engage in group reading activities with purpose and understanding.

READING INFORMATIONAL TEXT

RI.K.1—With prompting and support, ask and answer questions about key details in a text.

RI.K.2—With prompting and support, identify the main topic and retell key details of a text.

RI.K.3—With prompting and support, describe the connection between two individuals, events, ideas, or pieces of information in a text.

RI.K.4—With prompting and support, ask and answer questions about unknown words in a text.

RI.K.5—Identify the front cover, back cover, and title page of a book.

RI.K.6—Name the author and illustrator of a text and define the role of each in presenting the ideas or information in a text.

RI.K.7—With prompting and support, describe the relationship between illustrations and the text in which they appear (e.g., what person, place, thing, or idea in the text an illustration depicts).

RI.K.8—With prompting and support, identify the reasons an author gives to support points in a text.

RI.K.9—With prompting and support, identify basic similarities in and differences between two texts on the same topic (e.g., in illustrations, descriptions, or procedures).

RI.K.10—Actively engage in group reading activities with purpose and understanding.

READING: FOUNDATIONAL SKILLS

RF.K.1a—Follow words from left to right, top to bottom, and page by page.

RF.K.1b—Recognize that spoken words are represented in written language by specific sequences of letters.

RF.K.1d—Recognize and name all upper-and lower-case letters of the alphabet.

RF.K.2a—Recognize and produce rhyming words.

RF.K.2b—Count, pronounce, blend, and segment syllables in spoken words.

RF.K.2d—Isolate and pronounce the initial, medial vowel, and final sounds in three-phoneme (CVC) words (except words ending in /l/, /r/, or /x/).

RF.K.2e—Add or substitute individual sounds (phonemes) in simple, one-syllable words to make new words.

RF.K.3a—Demonstrate basic knowledge of one-to-one letter-sound correspondences by producing the primary or many of the most frequent sounds for each consonant.

RF.K.3b—Associate the long and short sounds with common spellings (graphemes) for the five major vowels.

RF.K.3c—Read common high-frequency words by sight (e.g., the, of, to, you, she, my, is, are, do, does).

RF.K.3d—Distinguish between similarly spelled words by identifying the sounds of the letters that differ.

RF.K.4—Read emergent reader texts with purpose and understanding.

WRITING

W.K.1—Use a combination of drawing, dictating, and writing to compose opinion pieces in which they tell a reader the topic or the name of the book they are writing about and state an opinion or preference about the topic or book (e.g., My favorite book is . . .).

W.K.2—Use a combination of drawing, dictating, and writing to compose informative and explanatory texts in which they name what they are writing about and supply some information about the topic.

W.K.3—Use a combination of drawing, dictating, and writing to narrate a single event or several loosely linked events, tell about the events in the order in which they occurred, and provide a reaction to what happened.

W.K.5—With guidance and support from adults, respond to questions and suggestions from peers and add details to strengthen writing as needed.

W.K.6—With guidance and support from adults, explore a variety of digital tools to produce and publish writing, including in collaboration with peers.

W.K.7—Participate in shared research and writing projects (e.g., explore a number of books by a favorite author and express opinions about them).

W.K.8—With guidance and support from adults, recall information from experiences or gather information from provided sources to answer a question.

SPEAKING AND LISTENING

SL.K.1a—Follow agreed-upon rules for discussions (e.g., listening to others and taking turns speaking about the topics and texts under discussion).

SL.K.1b—Continue a conversation through multiple exchanges.

SL.K.2—Confirm understanding of a text read aloud or information presented orally or through other media by asking and answering questions about key details and requesting clarification if something is not understood.

SL.K.3—Ask and answer questions in order to seek help, get information, or clarify something that is not understood.

SL.K.4—Describe familiar people, places, things, and events and, with prompting and support, provide additional detail.

SL.K.5—Add drawings or other visual displays to descriptions as desired to provide additional detail.

SL.K.6—Speak audibly and express thoughts, feelings, and ideas clearly.

LANGUAGE

L.K.1a—Print many upper- and lower-case letters.

L.K.1b—Use frequently occurring nouns and verbs.

L.K.1c—Form regular plural nouns orally by adding s or es (e.g., dog, dogs; wish, wishes).

L.K.1d—Understand and use question words (interrogatives) (e.g., who, what, where, when, why, how).

L.K.1e—Use the most frequently occurring prepositions (e.g., to, from, in, out, on, off, for, of, by, with).

L.K.1f—Produce and expand complete sentences in shared language activities.

L.K.2a—Capitalize the first word in a sentence and the pronoun I.

L.K.2b—Recognize and name end punctuation.

L.K.2c—Write a letter or letters for most consonant and short vowel sounds.

L.K.2d—Spell simple words phonetically, drawing on knowledge of sound-letter relationships.

L.K.4a—Identify new meanings for familiar words and apply them accurately (e.g., knowing a duck is a bird, and learning the verb duck).

L.K.4b—Use the most frequently occurring inflections and affixes (e.g., -ed, -s, re-, un-, pre-, -ful, -less) as a clue to the meaning of an unknown word.

L.K.5a—Sort common objects into categories to gain a sense of the concepts the categories represent (e.g., foods, shapes, animals, plants).

L.K.5b—Demonstrate understanding of frequently occurring verbs and adjectives by relating them to their opposites (antonyms).

L.K.5c—Identify real-life connections between words and their use (e.g., note places at school that are colorful).

L.K.5d—Distinguish shades of meaning among verbs describing the same general action (e.g., walk, march, strut, prance) by acting out the meanings.

L.K.6—Use words and phrases acquired through conversations, reading and being read to, and responding to text.

NOTE

A complete list of text exemplars, standards, and resource materials as identified by the National Governors Association Center for Best Practices can be found at http://corestandards.org/ELA-Literacy.

FOUR

Kindergarten Strategies and Activities for Reading Literature

Choose literary text from Grades K–1 Text Exemplars selections or other appropriate grade-level selections. Grade K–1 Exemplars are noted with an (EX). Students work individually, as partners, small groups, or as a class.

- Ask and answer questions about key details. (RL.K.1, RL.K.3, RL.K.6, RI.K.1, RI.K.2, RI.K.3, RI.K.6, SL.K.2, SL.K.3)
- Use narrative and problem solution frames when asking and answering questions about literary texts. (RL.K.1, RL.K.2, RL.K.3)
- Use a 5W and How chart and/or a T-chart to compare and contrast literature (prose and poetry). (RL.K.1, RL.K.3, RL.K.5, RL.K.9, L.K.1d)

  - Read various nursery rhymes and poems and classify the rhyming words.
  - Read to compare and contrast *Pancakes for Breakfast* (EX) by Tomie DePaola and "Mix a Pancake" (EX) by Christina Rossetti.
  - Read to compare and contrast *Frog and Toad Together* (EX) by Arnold Lobel and "Two Tree Toads" (EX) by Jon Agee.
  - Read to compare and contrast events in various Little Bear (EX) stories by Else Minarik.
  - Read to compare and contrast different versions of the Three Little Pigs.

    - *Three Little Pigs* by Patricia Seibert (2000)
    - *The Three Little Pigs* by James Marshall (1996)

23

- *The True Story of the Three Little* Pigs by Jon Scieszka (1996)

- Use KWL charts to summarize what students know. Facilitate discussion and complete the chart, identifying what students want to know and what they have learned at the end of the unit. Then use the information from the chart to create class or group explanatory and informative summaries. (RL.K.1, RI.K.1, W.K.2, W.K.3, L.K.6)
- Use graphic organizers such as webs or maps and 5W and How to organize information such as story/character/setting; beginning/middle/end of stories; or informational texts to summarize. (RL.K.1, RL.K.2, RL.K.3, RI.K.1, RI.K.2, RI.K.3)

  - Summarize Mercer Mayer's *A Boy, a Dog, and a Frog* (EX).
  - Use a web to summarize John Langstaff's *Over in the Meadow* (EX).

- Read stories and poems with adult support identifying characters, settings, and major events. (RL.K.1, RL.K.2, RL.K.3, RL.K.10, SL.K.3)
- Play summary ball by throwing a small ball to a student and asking a who, what, where, when, why, or how question related to story content; student responds and tosses the ball back to teacher. (RL.K.1, RL.K.2)
- Use the Kagan Cooperative Learning strategy called Snowball.[1] (RL.K.1, RL.K.2, RL.K.3, RL.K.6, RL.K.7, RI.K.1, RI.K.2, RI.K.3, RI.K.4, RI.K.5, RI.K.6, RI.K.7, RI.K.8, RF.K.1d, RF.K.2a, RF.K.3c, SL.K.1a, SL.K.1b, SL.K.4, SL.K.6, L.K.2b, L.K.4a, L.K.5b)

  - Use ping pong balls, whiffle balls, tennis balls, or other lightweight balls that can be tossed in the classroom so as not to waste paper when you want students to simply pair up; number or letter the balls so that there are two of each number or letter. You may also want to use symbols on the snowballs.
  - Until younger students can read questions, use numbers or letters on the snowballs and have students pair up that way. For example, you have snowballs in green and yellow; number a green and yellow with number 3. Have students toss the balls into the air as though it were "snowing." When the balls are tossed, each student takes a snowball and locates their corresponding number. For example, the number 3s pair up. Ask a question to green number 3. Yellow number 3 may help if help is requested. Then ask a question to yellow number 3. Green number 3 may help if help is requested. When all snowball pairs have responded, toss again and repeat the process.

- Teacher could ask each pair a question and the two could converse and decide upon an answer.
- Ask questions about key details, characters, events, and settings in stories; authors and illustrators; new words; letters of the alphabet; rhyming words; nouns and verbs; end punctuation.

- Draw three pictures to illustrate the beginning, middle, and end of a story; use the pictures to summarize a story or event. Write a few words or a sentence to tell what part of the story each picture represents. (RL.K.2, RL.K.7)
- Use illustrated time lines to retell stories indicating the beginning, middle, and end of stories with details. (RL.K.2)

  - Students can create a mural time line and add pictures to represent events in the story.

- Create a graphic organizer such as a web or map to organize ideas about characters, setting, details, and events in stories or two texts on the same topic; indicate the name of the author, illustrator, and title on the web. The webs can then be used to compare and contrast the stories or texts. (RL.K.2, RL.K.3, RL.K.6, RL.K.9, RI.K.2, RI.K.6)

  - *My Five Senses* by Margaret Miller (1998) and *My Five Senses* by Aliki (EX)
  - *Follow the Water from Brook to Ocean* by Arthur Dorros (EX) and *Water, Water Everywhere* by Cynthia Overbeck Bix and Mark Rauzon (EX)

- Hypothesize and test: What would happen if key details changed? Change a couple of details in the story and see if the changes affect the ending. (RLK.2, RI.K.2)
- Use a T-chart to classify favorite stories or poems. (RL.K.2)
- Use sticky notes, whiteboards, or chart paper to dictate, write, or illustrate key details and main ideas; use details later to compose group or class narrative or informational summaries. (RL.K.2, RL.K.3, RI.K.2, W.K.2, W.K.3, L.K.6)
- Write, dictate, or draw pictures to summarize adventures and experiences of characters in familiar stories or the main topic and key details in informational text. (RL.K.2, RI.K.2, W.K.3, W.K.6, W.K.8, L.K.6)
- Use writing and/or draw pictures on tri-folds to illustrate the beginning, middle, and end of stories; then use the information to create group or class summaries. (RL.K.2, RI.K.2, W.K.3, W.K.6, W.K.8, L.K.6)

- When listening to or reading literary or informational texts, students can "take notes" by writing or dictating responses to identify who, what, when, where, why, and how. Create a 5W and How chart for each reading. Use charts to compare and contrast literary or informational texts. (RL.K.2, RL.K.9, RI.K.2, RI.K.9, L.K.1d)
- Hypothesize and test: What would happen if a character changed, such as male to female/female to male; young to old/old to young? (RL.K.2, RL.K.3)
- Hypothesize and test: What would happen if the setting changed, such as different countries, states, cities, time of year, years, or centuries? (RL.K.2, RI.K.2, RI.K.3)
- Role-play familiar stories to retell stories to the class. (RL.K.2)
- Use T-charts and Venn diagrams to compare and contrast the adventures and experiences in stories and poems, types of texts (storybooks and poems), details, and between two nonfictional texts on the same topic. (RL.K.3, RL.K.5, RL.K.9, RI.K.9)
- Draw or role-play stories about things you see or events that happen or to describe familiar people, places, things, or events; use illustrations or other visual displays when speaking. (RL.K.3, RI.K.2, SL.K.4, SL.K.5, SL.K.6)
- Create illustrated time lines to depict favorite stories; describe the relationship between illustrations and the story or text being illustrated. (RL.K.3, RL.K.7, RI.K.2, RI.K.7)
- Create illustrated book covers, bookmarks, posters, or banners to describe favorite books or characters, stories, events, or scenes from favorite stories or books; identify the author and illustrator. (RL.K.3, RL.K.6, RI.K.2, RI.K.6, L.K.2)
- Use T-charts, category boxes, and Venn diagrams to identify and classify details, characters, settings, events, types of texts, rhyming words, words with long and short vowel sounds, upper- and lower-case letters, new meanings for familiar words, common objects, and opposites of verbs and adjectives. (RL.K.3, RL.K.5, RF.K.2a, RF.K.3b, L.K.1a, L.K.4a, L.K.5a, L.K.5b)
- Hypothesize and test: What happens if we do not ask for help with unknown words? (RL.K.4, RI.K.4)
- Ask and answer questions about unknown words. (RL.K.4, RI.K.4)
  - Use a definition frame in a group setting to define new words.
- Use the Kagan Cooperative Learning strategy called Find My Rule[2]. (RL.K.5, RF.K.1d, RF.K.2a, SL.K.1, SL.K.3, SL.K.6, L.K.1a–d, L.K.2a, L.K.5a–b)
  - Teacher lists various items on the whiteboard or overhead or chart to give students practice identifying the rule. For exam-

ple, list the words "cat," "hat," and "bat." Show one part of the rule at a time. The rule would be words that rhyme or short vowel sound for "a."

- Use sorted lists of words and phrases that suggest feelings or appeal to the senses; titles or storybooks or poems; words requiring capitalization; words with long or short vowel sounds, upper- and lower-case letters; singular and plural nouns with matching verbs.

- Use the Kagan Cooperative Learning strategy called Team-Pair-Solo[3]. (RL.K.5, RI.K.5, RF.K.1d, RF.K.2a, RF.K.3b, SL.K.1, SL.K.3, SL.K.6, L.K.1a–c, L.K.1f, L.K.2a–b, L.K.5a)

  - Students work together as a team of four until all students understand the concept. Students then work in pairs to complete similar tasks, with each partner checking the work of the other. Then students complete similar tasks on their own. For example, the team works together to understand how to write words that rhyme with "can"; then pairs write other words that rhyme; then students write rhyming pairs on their own.
  - When using groups of three, have groups sit close to each other so when the group breaks into pairs, new pairs are easily formed without too much movement or class disruptions. You might want to practice pairing up before implementing content.

    - Students practice skills of recognizing storybooks and poems; identifying text features; writing and naming upper- and lower-case letters; producing rhyming words; identifying words with long and short vowel sounds; using and forming singular and plural nouns and verbs; producing and expanding complete sentences; capitalizing first words and the pronoun "I"; recognizing and naming end punctuation; sorting common objects.

- Practice identifying author and illustrator of books and describe their roles. (RL.K.6, RI.K.6)
- Let each student identify his or her favorite story (you may wish to narrow the choices down to five or so). Students draw, dictate, or write an opinion piece naming the story, author, illustrator, and stating why the student liked it. Group students according to their choices. Each group will compare and contrast the opinions and will then write an opinion piece that expresses why each member likes the story and uses various digital tools to produce and publish

the opinion piece. (RL.K.6, W.K.1, W.K.6, W.K.7, SL.K.1a, SL.K.1b, SL.K.5, SL.K.6, L.K.6)

- Do a book-, story-, or poem-talk. The teacher has a basket of items representative of characters, events, and/or settings from various literary or informational readings. A student will choose an item from the basket and tell the class the name of the reading and what the object represents. (RL.K.7, RI.K.7, SL.K.6)
- Look at the illustrations and predict what will happen. (RL.K.7, RI.K.7)
- Describe the relationships between illustrations and the story and illustrations and the text. (RL.K.7, RI.K.7)
- Create an object display for favorite authors or favorite stories. Ask students what three things they would use to represent the story, poem, or author and why. Find as many items or representative pictures as possible and create the displays for various stories, poems, or authors. (This would be good to have students share with parents during conferences; students could explain the signifi-cance of the items to the parents.) (RL.K.7, RI.K.7, SL.K.6)
- Compare and contrast the adventures of characters or events set in different countries. (RL.K.9, RI.K.9)

  - Read various versions of Little Red Riding Hood including an original version and Ed Young's *Lon Po Po: A Red-Riding Hood Story from China* (EX).

- Actively engage in group reading activities with purpose and understanding. (RL.K.10, RI.K.10, L.K.6)

  - Listen to favorite stories on tape or have students record fa-vorite stories for others to hear.
  - Create a dance or special movement when listening to stories or poems with repetitive lines or words.
  - Let students create their own grammar rock songs—you can find the original Grammar Rock songs from the 1970s on YouTube or at Amazon.com (various).

- Students can move or clap hands to the beat of poems or when identifying syllables in words. (RL.K.10, RF.K.2b, RF.K.4)
- Predict what actions the character will take based on what you have read so far. (RL.K.10)
- When you reach the middle of the book, predict how it will end. (RL.K.10, RI.K.10)
- How does the main character react to events in the book? Hypothe-size about how others would react based on what you know of the other characters. (RL.K.10, RI.K.10)

- Read and/or listen to various versions of the same topics. Ask students to offer hypotheses about an issue in the stories and try to establish evidence to prove their hypotheses. (RL.K.10, RI.K.10)

  - *Christopher Columbus* by Stephen Krensky (1991) and *My First Biography: Christopher Columbus* by Marion Dane Bauer (2010)
  - *George Washington for Kids: His Life and Times with 21 Activities* by Brandon Marie Miller (2007) and *George Washington and the General's Dog* by Frank Murphy (2002)
  - *Lewis and Clark: A Prairie Dog for the President* by Shirley Raye Redmond and John Manders (2003) and *Lewis and Clark for Kids: Their Journey of Discovery with 21 Activities* by Janis Herbert (2000)
  - *The True Story of Pocahontas* by Lucille Rech Penner (1994) and *Pocahontas: An American Princess* by Joyce Milton (2000)

- Use Golden Books to create literary kits—each kit contains a book, an artifact or two that are representative of the story, and a list of questions parents are to ask about the story as the child reads or is read to. You could also include a writing page of words so students can practice spelling or writing. Trade off each week or two so that all children get to read each book. Vary the genre, too. (RL.K.10)

NOTES

1. Kagan, S., & Kagan, M., "Kagan Cooperative Learning Smart Card" (San Clemente, 1997), 2–3.
2. See Kagan, S., & Kagan, M. (1997) for further information.
3. See Kagan, S., & Kagan, M. (1997) for further information.

FIVE

Kindergarten Strategies and Activities for Reading Informational Text

Choose informational text from Grades K–1 Text Exemplars selections or other appropriate grade-level selections. Grade K–1 Exemplars are noted with an (EX). Students work individually, as partners, small groups, or as a class.

- Use a 5W and How chart to compare and contrast two texts on the same topic. (RI.K.1, RI.K.2, RI.K .9, L.K.1d)

  - Clyde Bulla's *A Tree Is a Plant* (EX) and Wendy Pfeffer's *From Seed to Pumpkin* (EX)

- Read informational text with adult support to identify key details and main topics. (RI.K.1, RI.K.2, RI.K.3, RI.K.10)
- Draw three pictures to illustrate the beginning, middle, and end of an event; use the pictures to summarize a story or event. Write a few words or a sentence to tell what part of the story each picture represents. (RI.K.2, RI.K.7)
- Use analogies to help make connections between things that seem very different. Analogies help explain unfamiliar concepts by making a comparison to something that is understood. Teacher-directed analogies can be used two ways: the teacher can create the analogy and ask students to determine the concept or the teacher creates 75 percent of the analogy and asks the students to complete the analogy. (RI.K.3, L.K.1b, L.K.5a)

  - Create analogies using antonyms of frequently occurring verbs and adjectives (e.g., hot is to cold as dark is to light; run is to walk as go is to stop).

- Create analogies using words that rhyme (e.g., cat is to hat as boy is to toy; fun is to sun as hit is to mitt).

- Ask and answer questions about unknown words in a text. (RI.K.4)
- Practice identifying the front cover, back cover, and title page of a book. (RI.K.5)
- Practice identifying the author and illustrator of a text; define the role of each. (RI.K.6)
- Read and/or listen to informative texts about community helpers; use various graphic organizers to compare and contrast what they do. (RI.K.9)

  - Read *Fire! Fire!* (EX) and *Post Office* by Gail Gibbons.
  - Read *Jobs People Do* by Christopher Maynard.
  - *Berenstain Bears Go to the Doctor* by Stan and Jan Berenstain
  - *I Want to Be a Nurse* by Daniel Liebman
  - *I Want to Be a Teacher* by Daniel Liebman
  - *I Want to Be a Vet* by Daniel Liebman
  - *Career Day* by Anne Rockwell

- Use a T-chart to identify key points in a text and let students supply reasons given by the author for the key points. (RI.K.8)
- Create a list of all of the animals in the K–1 exemplars read in Kindergarten. Sort or classify animals into categories such as those with feathers, fur, neither; those that can fly or swim or are land or water animals. Talk about the similarities and differences of all the animals. Students participate in shared research to create an ABC of Nature book. Each student will choose one animal (number may vary depending on class size and the stories and poems read) and will research to find information about the animal—most likely from the materials read in class. Use digital tools to publish the book and create copies for each student to take home to read to an adult. (RI.K.9, W.K.2, W.K.6, W.K.7, SL.K.1a, SL.K.1b, SL.K.5, SL.K.6, L.K.6)

SIX

Kindergarten Strategies and Activities for Reading Foundational Skills

Choose literary and informational text from Grades K–1 Text Exemplars selections or other appropriate grade-level selections. Grade K–1 Exemplars are noted with an (EX). Students work individually, as partners, small groups, or as a class.

- Practice reading left to right at home and at school. (RF.K.1a)
- Practice naming and writing upper- and lower-case letters. (RF.K.1d, L.K.1a)

    - If you can handle the mess, use a cookie sheet and a small amount of sugar or sand; students can write the letters in the sugar or sand.
    - Practice writing letters on lined paper with and without letters printed on the page; practice writing their names as well on lined paper.

- Choose a letter of the day and have students practice writing words that begin with that letter. (RF.K.1d, L.K.2a)

    - Write students' names that begin with that letter; allow for capitalization practice, too.
    - You may wish to include words or names that contain the letter of the day to practice lower-case writing and recognition.

- Practice recognizing and producing rhyming words. (RF.K.2a)

    - Create word walls to illustrate words with long and short vowel sounds; add to the wall when students learn new rhyming words.

- Read various nursery rhymes and poems and classify the rhyming words by sound. (RF.K.2a)

  "Hey Diddle Diddle"
  "Humpty Dumpty"
  "Jack and Jill"
  "Jack Be Nimble"
  "Little Bo Peep"
  "Little Boy Blue"
  "Little Jack Horner"
  "Little Miss Muffet"
  "Old Mother Hubbard"
  "Ring Around the Rosie"
  "Rock-a-Bye, Baby"
  "Roses Are Red"
  "Simple Simon"
  "Star Light, Star Bright"

- Practice vocabulary words by saying the words and counting out syllables. (RF.K.2b, RF.K.2d)
- Sort vocabulary/spelling words by their respective spellings (such as vowel sounds, number of syllables, etc.). (RF.K.2b, RF.K.3b, L.K.4a)
- Practice reading high-frequency words. (RF.K.3c)
- Role-play emergent readers with purpose and understanding. (RF.K.4, SL.K.2)

SEVEN

Kindergarten Strategies and Activities for Writing

Choose literary and informational text from Grades K–1 Text Exemplars selections or other appropriate grade-level selections. Grade K–1 Exemplars are noted with an (EX). Students work individually, as partners, small groups, or as a class.

- Participate in shared research and group activities when appropriate. (W.K.1, W.K.6, W.K.7, SL.K.1a, SL.K.1b, SL.K.2, SL.K.6, L.K.6)

    - Complete and use information from KWL and 5W and How charts to participate in shared research and writing projects; take notes together as a group using writing, drawing, and/or dictating.
    - As a group, explore books by favorite authors and write, draw, or dictate opinions about the topics or books.

- Practice drawing, writing, and dictating to compose various writing pieces in which you write and expand sentences; include capital letters and appropriate end punctuation. (W.K.1, W.K.2, W.K.3, L.K.1f, L.K.2a, L.K.2b)
- Practice using nouns and verbs, question words, and prepositions in speaking and writing. (W.K.1, W.K.2, W.K.3, SL.K.2, SL.K.3, SL.K.4, SL.K.6, L.K.1b, L.K.1c, L.K.1d, L.K.1e)
- Work in small groups to draw, dictate, or write informative/explanatory texts, narrate single or loosely linked events. (W.K.2, W.K.3, SL.K.1, SL.K.6)

    - Create a class mural about a key event.
    - Retell and record a collection of published or original stories or poems on tape for other class members to enjoy.

- Hypothesize and test: What would happen if the order of events changed? (W.K.3)
- With guidance and support from adults, respond to questions and suggestions from peers and add details to strengthen writing as needed. (W.K.5)
- Ask and answer questions to strengthen writing. (W.K.5)
- When working in small groups, respond to questions and suggestions from adults and peers and add detail to strengthen writing. (W.K.5, SL.K.1, SL.K.6)
- Practice decision-making skills: What should we use to produce and publish our writings? (W.K.6)
- Practice decision-making skills: How often should we publish? (W.K.6)
- Practice decision-making skills: How will we distribute our publication? (W.K.6)
- Practice decision-making skills: What problems might we have? (W.K.6)
- Practice decision-making skills: How will we work around the problems? (W.K.6)
- Participate in shared research and group activities when appropriate. (W.K.6, W.K.7, SL.K.1a, SL.K.1b, SL.K.2, SL.K.6, L.K.6)
- Ask and answer questions to help generate hypotheses when participating in shared research and writing projects. (W.K.7)
- Participate in shared research and writing projects. (W.K.7, SL.K.1, SL.K.6)

  - Research favorite authors and their stories or poems; tell the class what you found.

- When working in small groups and with guidance and support from adults, recall information from experiences or gather information from provided sources to answer a question. (W.K.8, SL.K.1, SL.K.6)

EIGHT

Kindergarten Activities and Strategies for Speaking and Listening

Choose literary and informational text from Grades K–1 Text Exemplars selections or other appropriate grade-level selections. Grade K–1 Exemplars are noted with an (EX). Students work individually, as partners, small groups, or as a class.

- Participate in collaborative conversations with diverse partners with peers and adults in small and larger groups. (SL.K.1, SL.K.6)
- Hypothesize and test: What happens if we do not follow rules or class procedures? (SL.K.1a, SL.K.1b)
- Ask and answer questions to participate in collaborative conversations. (SL.K.1a, SL.K.1b)
- Ask and answer questions to get clarification and information. (SL.K.3)

  - Encourage students to not only ask you for clarification and information but also classmates when working in group situations.

- With prompting and support, describe familiar people, places, things, and events to help in group discussions. (SL.K.4, SL.K.6)

  - As students read or listen to stories, encourage them to share information about people, places, things, or events similar to those in the story; for example, if you read a story about a park, ask students to describe the people they saw (park rangers), special places like the walking paths or fountains, the different attractions in the park (bird cages), and special events that took place there.

Chapter 8

- Practice verbally describing people, places, things, and events and provide additional detail. (SL.K.4)

    - Ask students to stand and describe: the day's weather, classmates, the lunch room, favorite holidays, etc., beginning with two to three details and expanding to as many as possible.

- Add drawings or visual displays to descriptions to provide additional detail. (SL.K.5)

    - As students work with description, have them draw a picture of the item to be described; then share each detail verbally with the class.

- Hypothesize and test: What happens if we do not speak clearly in class? (SL.K.6)

    - Role-play a situation where a student does not speak clearly and another does; ask students about the situation.

- Speak clearly and audibly so that cues will be picked up by everyone. (SL.K.6)

NINE

Kindergarten Strategies and Activities for Language

Choose literary and informational text from Grades K–1 Text Exemplars selections or other appropriate grade-level selections. Grade K–1 Exemplars are noted with an (EX). Students work individually, as partners, small groups, or as a class.

- Practice writing upper- and lower-case letters. (L.K.1a)

    - Using an Alphabox, let students practice vocabulary words by writing the words in the correct box.
    - Create an alphabet booklet each quarter; staple sheets of lined paper together and write a letter of the alphabet on each side. As new words are learned, have the student write the new word on the page. Send the booklets home at the end of the quarter so students can practice reading and spelling the words. (You could also read the booklets aloud when you have a few extra moments.)

- Use frequently occurring nouns and verbs in speaking and writing. (L.K.1b)
- Practice creating and writing plural nouns by adding "s" or "es." (L.K.1c)
- Use question words when talking about literary and informational pieces. (L.K.1d)

    - Refer to 5W and How charts when working with question words.

- Practice following directions. (L.K.1e)

- Ask students to demonstrate how to walk to, from, in, out, on, off, for, by something or someone in the classroom.
- Whisper a direction to a student and ask the class to guess what the student is doing.

- Produce and expand complete sentences in shared language activities. (L.K.1f)

  - Write a simple sentence on the board; allow students to add detail words to expand the sentence, rewriting the sentence each time.

- Capitalize the first word in sentences and the pronoun "I." (L.K.2a)
- Practice naming end punctuation. (L.K.2b)

  - Create flashcards of punctuation for students to take home for practice.
  - Ask students to verbally give you a sentence that ends with a specific type of punctuation.

- Write a letter or letters for most consonant and short vowel sounds. (L.K.2c)
- Practice spelling words phonetically. (L.K.2d)

  - If parents have the magnetic letters at home, encourage students to practice on a magnetic surface.

- Identify new meanings for familiar words and apply them accurately. (L.K.4a)

  - Create a wall chart for homophones; add new words as they come up in class discussion or reading; begin with some of these: ant-aunt, ate-eight, bear-bare, bee-be, by-buy, choose-chews, flew-flu, flower-flour, hair-hare, whole-hole, horse-hoarse, I-eye, meet-meat, new-knew, one-won, our-hour, plane-plain, red-read, sail-sale, see-sea, tail-tale, to-two-too, wood-would, you-ewe.
  - Create flashcards for new pairs as they are introduced and encourage students to verbally create sentences using the new word.

- Practice sorting common objects. (L.K.5a)
- Practice identifying antonyms of verbs and adjectives. (L.K.5b)

  - Create sets of flash cards with verbs and adjectives; for each word, write the antonym on the back. Students can work with parents as they read the word and give the antonym.

- Use words and phrases acquired in reading and conversations, reading and being read to, and responding to texts. (L.K.6)

TEN

Grade 1 Common Core State Standards

READING LITERATURE

RL.1.1—Ask and answer questions about key details in a text.

RL.1.2—Retell stories, including key details, and demonstrate understanding of their central message or lesson.

RL.1.3—Describe characters, settings, and major events in a story, using key details.

RL.1.4—Identify words and phrases in stories or poems that suggest feelings or appeal to the senses.

RL.1.5—Explain major differences between books that tell stories and books that give information, drawing on a wide reading of a range of text types.

RL.1.6—Identify who is telling the story at various points in a text.

RL.1.7—Use illustrations and details in a story to describe its characters, setting, or events.

RL.1.9—Compare and contrast the adventures and experiences of characters in stories.

RL.1.10—With prompting and support, read prose and poetry of appropriate complexity for grade 1.

READING INFORMATIONAL TEXT

RI.1.1—Ask and answer questions about key details in a text.

RI.1.2—Identify the main topic and retell key details of a text.

RI.1.3—Describe the connection between two individuals, events, ideas, or pieces of information in a text.

RI.1.4—Ask and answer questions to help determine or clarify the meaning of words and phrases in a text.

RI.1.5—Know and use various text features (e.g., headings, tables of contents, glossaries, electronic menus, icons) to locate key facts or information in a text.

RI.1.6—Distinguish between information provided by pictures or other illustrations and information provided by the words in a text.

RI.1.7—Use the illustrations and details in a text to describe its key ideas.

RI.1.8—Identify the reasons an author gives to support points in a text.

RI.1.9—Identify basic similarities in and differences between two texts on the same topic (e.g., in illustrations, descriptions, or procedures).

RI.1.10—With prompting and support, read informational texts appropriately complex for grade 1.

READING: FOUNDATIONAL SKILLS

RF.1.1a—Recognize the distinguishing features of a sentence (e.g., first word, capitalization, ending punctuation).

RF.1.2a—Distinguish long from short vowel sounds in spoken single-syllable words.

RF.1.2b—Orally produce single-syllable words by blending sounds, including consonant blends.

RF.1.2c—Isolate and pronounce initial, medial vowel, and final sounds in spoken single-syllable words.

RF.1.2d—Segment spoken single-syllable words into their complete sequence of individual sounds.

RF.1.3b—Decode regularly spelled one-syllable words.

RF.1.3e—Decode two-syllable words following basic patterns by breaking the words into syllables.

RF.1.3f—Read words with inflectional endings.

RF.1.3g—Recognize and read grade-appropriate irregularly spelled words.

RF.1.4a—Read on-level text with purpose and understanding.

RF.1.4b—Read on-level text orally with accuracy, appropriate rate, and expression on successive readings.

RF.1.4c—Use context to confirm or self-correct word recognition and understanding, rereading as necessary.

WRITING

W.1.1 — Write opinion pieces in which they introduce the topic or name the book they are writing about, state an opinion, supply a reason for the opinion, and provide some sense of closure.

W.1.2 — Write informative/explanatory texts in which they name a topic, supply some facts about the topic, and provide some sense of closure.

W.1.3 — Write narratives in which they recount two or more appropriately sequenced events, include some details regarding what happened, use temporal words to signal event order, and provide some sense of closure.

W.1.5 — With guidance and support from adults, focus on a topic, respond to questions and suggestions from peers, and add details to strengthen writing as needed.

W.1.6 — With guidance and support from adults, use a variety of digital tools to produce and publish writing, including in collaboration with peers.

W.1.7 — Participate in shared research and writing projects (e.g., explore a number of "how-to" books on a given topic and use them to write a sequence of instructions).

W.1.8 — With guidance and support from adults, recall information from experiences or gather information from provided sources to answer a question.

SPEAKING AND LISTENING

SL.1.1a — Follow agreed-upon rules for discussions.

SL.1.1b — Build on others' talk in conversations by responding to the comments of others through multiple exchanges.

SL.1.1c — Ask questions to clear up any confusion about the topics and texts under discussion.

SL.1.2 — Ask and answer questions about key details in a text read aloud or information presented orally or through other media.

SL.1.3 — Ask and answer questions about what a speaker says in order to gather additional information or clarify something that is not understood.

SL.1.4 — Describe people, places, things, and events with relevant details, expressing ideas and feelings clearly.

SL.1.5 — Add drawings or other visual displays to descriptions when appropriate to clarify ideas, thoughts, and feelings.

SL.1.6 — Produce complete sentences when appropriate to task and situation.

LANGUAGE

L.1.a—Print all upper- and lower-case letters.

L.1.b—Use common, proper, and possessive nouns.

L.1.c—Use singular and plural nouns with matching verbs in basic sentences (e.g., he hops; we hop).

L.1.d—Use personal, possessive, and indefinite pronouns (e.g., I, me, my; they, them, their; anyone, everything).

L.1.e—Use verbs to convey a sense of past, present, and future (e.g., yesterday I walked home; today I walk home; tomorrow I will walk home).

L.1.f—Use frequently occurring adjectives.

L.1.g—Use frequently occurring conjunctions (e.g., and, but, or, so, because).

L.1.h—Use determiners (e.g., articles, demonstratives).

L.1.i—Use frequently occurring prepositions (e.g., during, beyond, toward).

L.1.j—Produce and expand complete simple and compound declarative, interrogative, imperative, and exclamatory sentences in response to prompts.

L.1.2a—Capitalize dates and names of people.

L.1.2b—Use end punctuation for sentences.

L.1.2c—Use commas in dates and to separate single words in a series.

L.1.2d—Use conventional spelling for words with common spelling patterns and for frequently occurring irregular words.

L.1.2e—Spell untaught words phonetically, drawing on phonemic awareness and spelling conventions.

L.1.4a—Use sentence-level context as a clue to the meaning of a word or phrase.

L.1.4b—Use frequently occurring affixes as a clue to the meaning of a word.

L.1.4c—Identify frequently occurring root words (e.g., look) and their inflectional forms (e.g., looked, looking).

L.1.5a—Sort words into categories (e.g., colors, clothing) to gain a sense of the concepts the categories represent.

L.1.5b—Define words by category and by one or more key attributes (e.g., a duck is a bird that swims; a tiger is a large cat with stripes).

L.1.5c—Identify real-life connections between words and their use (e.g., note places at home that are cozy).

L.1.5d—Distinguish shades of meaning among verbs differing in manner (e.g., look, peek, glance, stare, glare, scowl) and adjectives differing in intensity (e.g., large, gigantic) by defining or choosing them or by acting out the meanings.

L.1.6—Use words and phrases acquired through conversations, reading and being read to, and responding to texts, including using frequently occurring conjunctions to signal simple relationships (e.g., because).

NOTE

A complete list of text exemplars, standards, and resource materials as identified by the National Governors Association Center for Best Practices can be found at http://corestandards.org/ELA-Literacy.

ELEVEN

Grade 1 Strategies and Activities for Reading Literature

Choose literary text from Grades K–1 Text Exemplars selections or other appropriate grade-level selections. Grade K–1 Exemplars are noted with an (EX). Students work individually, as partners, small groups, or as a class.

- Use stem questions to ask about key details, characters, settings, events, ideas, and author's reasons. (RL.1.1, RL.1.2, RL.1.3, RL.1.7, SL.1.2, SL.1.3, SL.1.4)
- Create an acrostic from the title to create a summary of a story. (RL.1.1, RL.1.2, RL.1.3)
- Use 5W and How charts to practice retelling stories and asking and answering questions about key details, characters, settings, main topics, people, places, events, and things. (RL.1.1, RL.1.2, RL.1.3, RL.1.7)
- Use stem questions to help generate and test hypotheses and help students explain their results. (RL.1.1, RL.1.10)

    - Try books similar to or including:

        - *The Statue of Liberty* by Lucille Rech Penner (1995)
        - *Bones* by Stephen Krensky (1999)
        - *Dinosaur Babies* by Lucille Rech Penner (1991)

- Hypothesize and test: What would happen if key details changed? (RL.1.1, RL.1.2, RL.1.3, RI.1.1, RI.1.2)
- Hypothesize and test: What would happen if a character changed such as male to female/female to male; young to old/old to young? (RL.1.1, RL.1.2)

- Hypothesize and test: What would happen if the setting changed such as different countries, states, cities, times of year, years, or centuries? (RL.1.1, RL.1.3, RI.1.2, RI.1.3)
- Use the Kagan Cooperative Learning strategy called Snowball.[1] (RL.1.1, RL.1.2, RL.1.3, RL.1.4, RL.1.5, RL.1.7, RI.1.1, RI.1.2, RI.1.5, RF.1.1, RF.1.2a, L.1.1a–g, L.1.1j, L.1.2a–c, L.1.4a–c, L.1.5a–b)

  - You could use ping pong balls, whiffle balls, tennis balls, or other lightweight balls that can be tossed in the classroom so as not to waste paper when you want students to simply pair up; number or letter the balls so that there are two of each number or letter. You may also want to use symbols on the snowballs.
  - Until younger students can read questions, use numbers or letters on the snowballs and have students pair up that way. For example, you have snowballs in green and yellow; number a green and yellow with number 3. Have students toss the balls into the air as though it were "snowing." When the balls are tossed, each student takes a snowball and locates their corresponding number. For example, the number 3s pair up. Ask a question to green number 3. Yellow number 3 may help if help is requested. Then ask a question to yellow number 3. Green number 3 may help if help is requested. When all snowball pairs have responded, toss again and repeat the process.
  - When students are able to read questions or terms or definitions, allow them to draw a question or a term or definition from a "snowbowl."

    - Allow the pair to converse and decide upon an answer.
    - Ask questions about key details, illustrations, characters, events, and settings in stories; authors and illustrators; words and phrases in stories and poems that suggest feelings or appeal to the senses; text features; parts of a sentence; long and short vowel sounds in spoken words; upper- and lower-case letters; common, proper, and possessive nouns; singular and plural nouns and verbs; past, present, and future tense verbs; adjectives, conjunctions, and prepositions; simple and compound sentences; capitalization and punctuation; words with affixes; sort words into categories.

- Use an organizer to take notes on various stories about characters, settings, illustrations, adventures, experiences, and events; use the information to write or dictate summaries of narratives. (RL.1.2, RL.1.3, RL.1.7, RL.1.10, W.1.1, W.1.3, L.1.6)

- *Owl at Home* by Arnold Lobel (EX)
- *Finn Family Moomintroll* by Tove Jansson (EX)

- Use narrative, definition, and problem/solution summary frames with various texts. (RL.1.2, RL.1.3, RL.1.4)
- Use book titles to help write summaries or take notes. (RL1.2, RL.1.3, RL.1.7, RI.1.2, RI.1.7)

  - Have students write the title of the book or story down the page, one letter on each line. You may have to abbreviate the title if it is too long. Each letter on the line begins the word or phrase on the line. Students may write a word or phrase to note specific details from the story. You may also choose to use characters' names for characterizations. Here is an example using *Starfish* by Edith Thacher Hurd.

    - **S**tarfish live deep in the ocean
    - **T**hey can be purple or pink
    - **A**ll starfish have feet but no toes
    - **R**ays help it go up and down
    - **F**eeds on oysters, mussels, and clams
    - **I**t can break open a clam shell with its rays
    - **S**tarfish lay many, many eggs in the sea
    - **H**as no eyes, ears, or nose

- Create webs to retell stories with details about characters, settings, and events and describe people, places, things, or events; webs can then be used to write narratives or compare and contrast stories. (RL.1.2, RL.1.3, RL.1.9, W.1.2, W.1.3, SL.1.4, SL.1.5)
- Use illustrated tri-folds or time lines to retell stories with details indicating the beginning, middle, and end of stories. (RL.1.2)
- Do a book-, story-, or poem-talk. The teacher creates a basket of items representative of characters, events, and/or settings from various literary or informational readings. A student will choose an item from the basket and tell the class the name of the reading and what the object represents. (RL.1.2, RL.1.3, RI.1.2, SL.K.6)
- Compare and contrast various stories, characters, settings, illustrations, adventures, experiences, and events using various organizers. (RL.1.3, RL.1.9, RL.1.10)

  - *Berenstain Bears by the Sea* by Stan Berenstain and Jan Berenstain (1998) and *Berenstain Bears Catch the Bus* by Stan Berenstain and Jan Berenstain (1999)
  - *Friends Forever* by Melissa Lagonegro (2009) and *The Great Toy Escape* by Kitty Richards (2010)
  - *Mater and the Little Tractors* by Chelsea Eberly (2012) and *Mater's Birthday Surprise* by Melissa Lagonegro (2012)

- Create a chart to classify characters, settings, favorite stories, favorite authors, and major events. (RL.1.3, RL.1.9)
- Create illustrated book covers, bookmarks, posters, or banners to describe favorite books or characters, stories, events, or scenes from favorite stories or books. (RL.1.3, RI.1.2)
- Use word webs to describe connections between individuals, events, ideas, or pieces of information; identify details to create summaries. (RL.1.3, RL.1.7, RI.1.3, RI.1.7)
- Create a chart to identify and sort words and phrases that suggest feelings or appeal to senses; state the feeling or the sense. (RL.1.4)

  - *Owl at Home* by Arnold Lobel (EX)
  - *The Wonderful Wizard of Oz* by Frank Baum (EX)
  - *Little House in the Big Woods* by Laura Ingalls Wilder (EX)
  - *Kitten's First Full Moon* by Kevin Henkes (EX)
  - "April Rain Song" by Langston Hughes (EX)
  - *My Five Senses* by Aliki (EX)
  - *The Paper Crane* by Molly Bang (EX)

- Read or listen to a story or poem. Have students draw symbols or images to represent three feelings they have when reading or listening to the poem. (RL.1.4)
- Practice identifying words that suggest feelings or apply to the senses and create an illustrated chart to categorize each. (RL 1.4)
- Use the Kagan Cooperative Learning strategy called Find My Rule[2]. (RL.1.4, RI.1.5, RF.1.1a, RF.1.2a, L.1.1a–j, L.1.5a)

  - Teacher lists various items on the whiteboard or overhead or chart to give students practice identifying the rule. For example, list the words "walk," "run," and "jump." Show one part of the rule at a time. The rule would be common verbs.

    - Use sorted lists of words and phrases that suggest feelings or appeal to the senses; titles or storybooks or poems; text features; parts of a sentence; long and short vowel sounds; upper- and lower-case letters; common, proper, and possessive nouns; singular and plural nouns and verbs; personal, possessive, and indefinite pronouns; past, present, and future tense verbs; adjectives, conjunctions; words requiring capitalization; end punctuation.

- Create a T-chart to contrast books that tell stories and books that give information. (RL.1.5)
- Practice reading literary text at home. (RL.1.6, RL.1.10)

  - Students can also be asked to identify who is telling the story at various points in the text.

- Create illustrated time lines to depict stories, characters, settings, and events; then let students retell the stories from the time lines. (RL.1.7)
- Create tri-folds to illustrate key details that describe characters, setting, key ideas, or events. (RL.1.7)
- Look at the illustrations in the story and predict what will happen, how the characters will react, and where the story takes place; then read the story to check the prediction. (RI.1.7)
- Use 5W and How charts, Venn diagrams, or T-charts to practice comparing and contrasting adventures and experiences or to illustrate similarities and differences between texts on the same topics. (RL.1.9, RI.1.9)
- Compare and contrast prose and poetry. (RL.1.9, RL.1.10, RI.1.9, RI.1.10)

  - Compare *Owl at Home* by Arnold Lobel (EX) to "The Owl and the Pussycat" by Edward Lear (EX).

- Compare and contrast opinion pieces, narratives, informational, and explanatory pieces. (RL.1.9, RI.1.9, W.1.1, W.1.2, W.1.3)
- Use T-charts or Venn diagrams to compare and contrast adventures and experiences in texts. (RL.1.9)
- Read text or listen to favorite stories on tape and/or have students record their favorite stories for others to hear. (RL.1.10)

  - Try your local library or check the web for stories on tape.

    - www.kidslearnoutloud.com
    - www.growler.com

- Predict what actions the character will take based on what you have read so far. (RL.1.10)
- When you reach the middle of the book, predict how it will end. (RL.1.10, RI.1.10)
- How does the main character react to events in the book? Hypothesize about how others would react based on what you know of the other characters. (RL.1.10, RI.1.10)
- With prompting and support, read prose and poetry of appropriate complexity for grade 1. (RL.1.10)
- Read and/or listen to various versions of the same topics. Ask students to offer hypotheses about an issue in the stories and try to establish evidence to prove their hypotheses. (RL.1.10, RI.1.10)

  - Try these or other appropriate versions:

    - *Abe Lincoln's Hat* by Martha Brenner (1994)
    - *Honest Abe Lincoln: Easy to Read Stories about Abraham Lincoln* by David Adler (2009)

- *Abraham Lincoln* by Edgar Parin D'Aulaire and Ingri D'Aulaire (1987)
- *Martin Luther King, Jr., and the March on Washington* by Frances E. Ruffin (2000)
- *My First Biography: Martin Luther King, Jr.* by Marion Dane Bauer (2009)
- *A Picture Book of Martin Luther King, Jr.* by David Adler (1990)
- *Rosa Parks* by Courtney Baker (2004)
- *A Picture Book of Rosa Parks* by David Adler (1995)
- *I Am Rosa Parks* by James Haskins and Rosa Parks (1999)

- Use KWL charts to identify what students know, want to know, and what they have learned (various).
- Teach specific content in separate corners of the room when possible; use posters and pictures to help convey the content (various).

NOTES

1. Kagan, S., & Kagan, M., "Kagan Cooperative Learning Smart Card" (San Clemente, 1997), 2–3.
2. See Kagan, S., & Kagan, M. (1997) for further information.

TWELVE

Grade 1 Strategies and Activities for Reading Informational Text

Choose informational text from Grades K–1 Text Exemplars selections or other appropriate grade-level selections. Grade K–1 Exemplars are noted with an (EX). Students work individually, as partners, small groups, or as a class.

- Use stem questions to ask about key details, main topics, connections in information, meanings of words, textual features, how information is provided, use of illustrations and details in a text, supportive information, and to identify similarities and differences in two texts on the same topic. (RI.1.1, RI.1.2, RI.1.3, RI.1.4, RI.1.5, RI.1.6, RI.1.7, RI.1.8, RI.1.9, SL.1.2, SL.1.3, SL.1.4)
- Hypothesize and test: What would happen if key details changed? (RI.1.1, RI.1.2)
- Hypothesize and test: What would happen if the individuals changed? (RI.1.1, RI.1.2)
- Hypothesize and test: What would happen if ideas changed? (RI.1.1, RI.1.2)
- Use 5W and How charts to practice asking and answering questions about key details in a text, identifying the main topic, and retelling key details. (RI.1.1, RI.1.2, RI.1.7)
- Use definition and problem/solution frames with various informational texts. (RI.1.2, RI.1.4)
- Use sticky notes, whiteboards, or chart paper to dictate, write, or illustrate key details, identify main topics, describe characters, settings and major events, and informative and explanatory text. (RI.1.2, RI.1.7, W.1.1, W.1.2, W.1.3, L.1.6)

- *A Weed Is a Flower: The Life of George Washington Carver* by Aliki (EX)
- *The Year at Maple Hill Farm* by Alice and Martin Provensen (EX)

- Create a graphic organizer such as a web or map to organize ideas about main topics and key details; identify similarities and differences in two texts on the same topic; describe connections between individuals, events, ideas, or information; prewrite informative or explanatory texts; and identify the reasons an author gives to support points in a text. The webs can then be used to compare and contrast the texts. (RI.1.2, RI.1.3, RI.1.8, RI.1.9, W.1.2)
- Create a Venn diagram to show how two people, events, ideas, or pieces of information are connected. (RI.1.3)
- Hypothesize and test: What happens if we do not ask for help with unknown words? (RI.1.4)
- Hypothesize and test: What happens if we do not get help with clarification and information? (RI.1.4)
- Create scavenger hunts to practice using textual features to locate facts or information. (RI.1.5)

  - Using various classroom textbooks, library books, and computers, create different sets of questions for groups that require students to find the answers in text features. Use different questions for each group of students. Make a game out of the scavenger hunt, trading questions among groups after each search is completed so that students have several opportunities to practice locating information using textual features.

- Create a T-chart labeled "Pictures/Illustrations" and "Information from Text." Use the chart to sort information found in the text; list the information on the appropriate side of the chart. (RI.1.6)
- Practice reading informational text at home to determine the purpose of the text—what the author wants to answer, explain, or describe. (RI.1.6, RI.1.10)

  - Students can also be asked to identify who is telling the story at various points in the text.
  - Create informational reading packets using excerpts from nonfiction text; include passages, excerpts, or small nonfiction books, guided questions for the parents to ask the student, representative artifacts (to pique interest in the story), and a response form for the student to complete with regard to author purpose.

- Look at the illustrations in the text and predict what the text is about; then read the text to check the prediction. (RI.1.7)
- After reading informational text, ask students to draw a picture that represents what they have read; ask students to share their information with the class to check for comprehension. (RI.1.7)
- Hypothesize and test: Why does the author make certain points in the text? Then identify the reasons he/she gives to support the points. (RI.1.8)
- Create webs or other graphic organizers to identify basic similarities and differences in texts on the same topic. (RI.1.9)
- With prompting and support, read informational text of appropriate complexity for grade 1. (RI.1.10)
- Create T-charts, webs, or Venn diagrams to compare and contrast informational texts on the same topic. (RI.1.9, RI.1.10)

  - Contrast *Starfish* by Edith Thacher Hurd (EX) and *Amazing Whales!* by Sarah L. Thompson (EX).

THIRTEEN

Grade 1 Strategies and Activities for Reading Foundational Skills

Choose literary and informational text from Grades K–1 Text Exemplars selections or other appropriate grade-level selections. Grade K–1 Exemplars are noted with an (EX). Students work individually, as partners, small groups, or as a class.

- Practice identifying first words, end punctuation, and capitalization in various literary and informational texts. (RF.1.1a, L.1.2a, L.1.2b)

  - Send home copies of "Wind Power" (*National Geographic Young Explorers*, November/December 2009) (EX) or other short, appropriate pieces of writing. Ask students to read the example with a parent or guardian and underline first words and words that are capitalized; circle end punctuation. Read and identify all parts the following day.

- Classify words with long or short vowel sounds and post on a word wall. (RF.1.2a)
- Create flashcards with single-syllable long and short vowel words; use at school and at home. (RF.1.2a)
- Practice identifying and pronouncing words with long and short vowel sounds—create a list or word wall of those you find. (RF.1.2a)
- Create analogies based on words with long and short vowel sounds and feeling words from stories and poems. (RF.1.2a)

  - Act out feeling words in the analogies.

- Create analogy activities from the following standards: RF.1.2a, L.1.1a, and L.1.1e.

- RF.1.2a Long/short vowels

  - Go is to show as tree is to _____.
  - Hat is to cat as hit is to _____.

- L.1.1a Upper- and lower-case letters

  - "A" is to "a" as "C" is to _____.
  - "g" is to _____ as "h" is to "H".

- L.1.1e Verb tense

  - Rode is to walked as climbed is to _____.
  - Ride is to walk as climb is to _____.
  - Will ride is to will walk as will climb is to _____.

- Orally produce single-syllable words by blending sounds, including consonant blends. (RF.1.2b)

  - Classify words with the same blends on webs or wall charts.

- Isolate and pronounce initial, medial vowel, and final sounds in spoken single-syllable words at home and at school. (RF.1.2c)
- Segment spoken single-syllable words into their complete sequence of individual sounds at home and at school. (RF.1.2d)
- Practice reading aloud and decoding one- and two-syllable words and grade-appropriate irregularly spelled words at home and at school. (RF.1.3b, RF.1.3e, RF.1.3g)

  - Create flashcards or word lists to use for practice.
  - Orally use the words in a sentence.

- Read on-level text with purpose and understanding at home and in the classroom. (RF.1.4a)
- Role-play on-level text with purpose and understanding. (RF.1.4a, RF.1.4b, RF.1.4c, SL.1.6)

  - Sway left and right to the beat while reading "Put Me in the Zoo" by Robert Lopshire (EX) or other appropriate poems such as "As I Was Going to St. Ives" by Anonymous (EX) or "By Myself" by Eloise Greenfield (EX).
  - Role-play the actions in "Over in the Meadow" by John Langstaff (EX) or other appropriate stories.

- Practice reading on-level text orally and self-correction. (RF.1.4a, RF.1.4b, RF.1.4c)

FOURTEEN

Grade 1 Strategies and Activities for Writing

Choose literary and informational text from Grades K–1 Text Exemplars selections or other appropriate grade level selections. Grade K–1 Exemplars are noted with an (EX). Students work individually, as partners, small groups, or as a class.

- After reading a selection, practice writing a sentence to express the topic or name of the book or story, tell whether or not you liked it, and give a reason why. (W.1.1, SL.1.6, L.1.6)
- Participate in shared research and writing projects. (W.1.2, W.1.3, W.1.5, W.1.6, W.1.7, W.1.8, SL.1.1a, SL.1.1b, SL.1.1c)
    - Create an ABC book for the class and have students research a topic to be produced and published.
        - Topics could include favorite stories or poems, authors, animals, or creatures.
        - Share the book with other classes or different grade levels.
- Practice choosing a topic (informative or explanatory), researching the topic and writing three details about the topic. (W.1.2, W.1.7, SL.1.6, L.1.6)
- Practice writing a story with three events in sequential order; include details, adjectives, temporal order words, a sense of closure, and appropriate end punctuation; add drawings where needed. (W.1.3, SL.1.5, SL.1.6, L.1.6)
- Create time lines to establish sequence of events and use the time lines to help write summaries. (W.1.3)
- Use time lines to help prewrite narratives. (W.1.3)

- Hypothesize and test: What would happen if the order of events changed? (W.1.3)
- Respond to questions from peers and adults to help improve writing and testing hypotheses. (W.1.5)
- Recall or gather information from various sources to strengthen writing. (W.1.5, W.1.8)
- Participate in shared research and group activities when appropriate. (W.1.6, W.1.7, SL.1.1a, SL.1.1b, SL.1.1c, SL.1.6, L.1.6)
- Participate in shared research and group activities when appropriate. (W.1.6, W.1.7, SL.1.1a, SL.1.1b, SL.1.1c, SL.1.6, L.1.6)

  - Complete and use information from KWL and 5W and How charts to participate in shared research and writing projects; take notes together as a group using writing, drawing, and/or dictating.
  - As a group, explore books by favorite authors and write, draw, or dictate notes about the topics or books.

- Practice decision-making skills: What should we use to produce and publish our ABC book? (W.1.6)
- Practice decision-making skills: How often should we publish? (W.1.6)
- Practice decision-making skills: How will we distribute our publication? (W.1.6)
- Practice decision-making skills: What problems might we have? (W.1.6)
- Practice decision-making skills: How will we work around the problems? (W.1.6)
- Recall or gather information from various sources about topics when participating in collaborative conversations during shared research and writing. (W.1.6, W.1.7, SL.1.1a, SL.1.1b, SL.1.1c)
- Use digital tools to write and publish your stories. (W.1.6, W.1.7)
- Practice writing directions to establish a sequence of instructions. (W.1.7)

  - How do you make a peanut butter and jelly sandwich?
  - How do you get to the playground or lunch room from the classroom?

- Use graphic organizers such as 5W and How charts or two-column notes when participating in shared research and writing projects to illustrate, dictate, or write summaries or notes. (W.1.7, SL.1.5)
- Ask and answer questions to help generate hypotheses when participating in shared research and writing projects. (W.1.7)
- Recall or gather information from various sources to generate and test hypotheses. (W.1.8)

FIFTEEN

Grade 1 Strategies and Activities for Speaking and Listening

Choose literary and informational text from Grades K–1 Text Exemplars selections or other appropriate grade-level selections. Grade K–1 Exemplars are noted with an (EX). Students work individually, as partners, small groups, or as a class.

- Participate in collaborative conversations using various strategies with diverse partners in small and large groups, taking turns and speaking clearly, and use acquired words. (SL.1.1a, SL.1.1b, SL.1.1c, SL.1.6, L.1.6)
- Hypothesize and test: What happens if we do not follow rules or class procedures? (SL.1.1a, SL.1.1b, SL.1.1c)
- Create grammar songs to help students create summaries or notes. (SL.1.4)
- Add drawings to narratives or informative or explanatory texts for clarification. (SL.1.5)
- Create a dance or special movement when listening to stories or poems with repetitive lines or words. (SL.1.5)

  - Read the story *Green Eggs and Ham* by Dr. Seuss (EX) or other Dr. Seuss stories. Have children create special movements to repeated lines (such as "I do not like green eggs and ham"). Reread the story with movements by the students.

- Use illustrations or other visual displays when speaking. (SL.1.5)
- Hypothesize and test: What happens if we do not speak clearly in class? (SL.1.6)
- Practice writing or verbalizing sentences. (SL.1.6, L.1.1b, L.1.1c, L.1.1d, L.1.1e)

- common, proper, and possessive nouns
- singular and plural nouns with matching verbs
- personal, possessive, and indefinite pronouns
- using verbs to convey past, present, and future

- Practice writing or verbalizing sentences with conjunctions and determiners and prepositions. (SL.1.6, L.1.1f, L.1.1g, L.1.1h, L.1.1i)
- Practice writing or verbalizing simple and compound declarative, interrogative, imperative, and exclamatory sentences. (SL.1.6, L.1.1j)

SIXTEEN

Grade 1 Strategies and Activities for Language

Choose literary and informational text from Grades K–1 Text Exemplars selections or other appropriate grade-level selections. Grade K–1 Exemplars are noted with an (EX). Students work individually, as partners, small groups, or as a class.

- Use the Kagan Cooperative Learning strategy called Team-Pair-Solo.[1] (L.1.1a-j, L.1.2a-c, L.1.5a)

  - Students work together as a team of four until all students understand the concept. Students then work in pairs to complete similar tasks, with each partner checking the work of the other. Then students complete similar tasks on their own. For example, the team works together to write a compound sentence; then pairs write a compound sentence; then students write their own compound sentence.
  - When using groups of three, have groups sit close to each other so when the group breaks into pairs, new pairs are easily formed without too much movement or class disruptions. You might want to practice pairing up before implementing content.

    - Students practice skills of identifying, writing, and using text features; upper- and lower-case letters; common, proper, and possessive nouns; singular and plural nouns and verbs; past, present, and future tense verbs; adjectives, conjunctions, and prepositions; simple and compound sentences; capitalization and punctuation;

words with affixes; sort words into categories working as a team, then pairs, then individually.

- Sort into categories and print upper- and lower-case letters. (L.1.1a)
  - Categories include upper-case, lower-case, rounded letters (such as a, b, c, d, e, g), stick letters (such as I, k, l), vowels, consonants.
- Practice writing all upper- and lower-case letters. (L.1.1a)
  - Can trace pre-printed letters on lined paper or write letters free hand.
  - Place sugar or sand on a cookie sheet and let students trace the letters.
- Write out groups of capital or lower-case letters such as "D-E-F" omitting one letter; ask students to supply the missing letter. (L.1.1a)
  - When students have mastered the skill, try groups of upper and lower-case letters such as "Dd-Ee-Ff"; omit one pair of letters and ask students to supply both.
- Create word scrambles from simple grade appropriate words. (L.1.1a)
- Choose five books and alphabetize the words in the titles. (L.1.1a)
- Students can lie down on the floor or stand in the shape of upper- and lower-case letters. (L.1.1a)
  - Form letters using bread dough or clay.
- Sort into categories common, proper, and possessive nouns using multicolumn T-chart. (L.1.1b)
- Sort into categories singular and plural nouns with matching verbs. (L.1.1c)
  - Create lists of singular and plural nouns; ask students to categorize each and then add a matching verb.
- Classify types of sentences and write examples of each with matching nouns and verbs. (L.1.1c, L.1.1j)
- Classify verbs according to past, present, and future tense using a graphic organizer or word wall. (L.1.1e)
- Create a "Word Bag." On notecards, write the grade appropriate adjectives, verbs, conjunctions, nouns, pronouns, past-present-future tense verbs, and prepositions. When you have "free time" allow one or more students to pull a word from the bag and use the word in a sentence. If you have time, write the sentence out in

lower case and ask students to add capitalization and punctuation. (L.1.1, L.1.2)

- You could also post the word on a word wall under the appropriate word classification. (L.1.5)

- Practice writing dates and people's names with capitalization. (L.1.2a)

- Capitalize the dates of special holidays or local celebrations.

- Write in lower case the names of people associated with favorite places in the community; ask students to capitalize the names. (L.1.2a)

- School principal, nurse, music teacher, etc.
- Local park, if named after someone
- TV characters
- Theme-park characters
- Favorite pets
- If you live in a smaller town, you might know the names of people who are associated with the grocery store, movie theaters, restaurants, etc.

- Write out students' names and birthdates in lower case; ask students to capitalize and punctuate (Lucy George, Wednesday, May 15, 2009). (L.1.2a, c)
- Practice end punctuation and commas in dates and listing single words in a series. (L.1.2b, L.1.2c)
- Practice writing and verbalizing spelling word lists. (L.1.2d)
- Classify words that rhyme in poetry. (L.1.5)

- "As I Was Going to St. Ives" by Anonymous (EX)
- "By Myself" by Eloise Greenfield (EX)

- Sort words into categories. (L.1.5a)

- Read *Are You My Mother?* by P. D. Eastman (EX). The hatchling asks animals and objects if they are his mother. Sort accordingly.

- Practice sorting words into categories and define words by category and key attributes. (L.1.5a, L.1.5b)

- *What Do You Do with a Tail Like This?* by Steve Jenkins and Robin Page (EX)

NOTE

1. Kagan, S., & Kagan, M., "Kagan Cooperative Learning Smart Card" (San Clemente, 1997), 2–3.

Appendix A: Alphabox

A	B	C	D
E	F	G	H
I	J	K	L
M	N	O	P
Q	R	S	T
U	V	W	XYZ

Appendix B: Summary Frames

NARRATIVE STORY FRAME

1. Who are the main characters and what are they like?
2. Where and when does the story take place?
3. What prompted the action in the story?
4. How did the characters express their feelings?
5. What did the main characters decide to do? If they set a goal, what was it?
6. How did the main characters try to accomplish their goal?
7. What were the consequences?

DEFINITION FRAME

1. What is being defined?
2. To which general category does the item belong?
3. What characteristics separate the item from other things in the general category?
4. What are some different types or classes of the item being defined?

PROBLEM/SOLUTION FRAME

1. What is the problem?
2. What is a possible solution?
3. What is another possible solution?
4. Which solution has the best chance of succeeding?

Appendix C: Stem Questions

Post these stem questions and statements in your classroom with your Verbs to Question list. Refer to both in classroom instruction as you work toward implementing higher-order questions in classroom instruction.

- Can you make a distinction between . . . ?
- Can you recall, name, select, list . . . ?
- Compare two like characters, people, events, places, or causes-effects.
- Could you explain your reasons?
- Define _____ using context clues.
- Describe the relationship between . . .
- Do you agree with the actions or outcome . . . ?
- Explain how . . .
- Explain the meaning of . . .
- Explain which clues from the text helped you understand the meaning.
- Give an example of . . .
- How did the title of _____ give a clue to the action/event that followed?
- How does _____? Support your answer.
- How does _____ compare/contrast with _____?
- How is _____ related to _____?
- How would you classify, compare, contrast . . . ?
- Identify the characteristics of . . .
- Label . . .
- List _____ major events in order.
- List the differences/similarities in . . .
- Show or explain the role of . . .
- What examples can you find . . . ?
- What facts or ideas show . . . ?
- What ideas can you add to . . . ?
- What is your opinion of . . . ?
- What was the most important event . . . ?
- What would be an example . . . ?
- Who, what, when, where, why . . . ?
- Why do you think . . . ?
- Why was the setting important . . . ?

Appendix D: Sample Kindergarten Advance Organizers

Create advance organizers for new stories or new informational text and share with students prior to reading. Advance organizers can help to establish characters, settings, details, events, connections in information, and similarities and differences in texts that students are about to read or events in which students are going to participate. (RL.K.1, RL.K.2, RL.K.3, RL.K.4, RL.K.6, RI.K.1, RI.K.2, RI.K.3, RI.K.8)

Use advance organizers like:

- KWL charts
- Flowcharts
- Outlines
- Webs—descriptive, concept
- SQRRR strategies
- 5W and How
- Alphaboxes

Use expository advance organizers to describe the new content to be learned. Here is an example:

Mrs. Sandy's Kindergarten class is studying seeds and plants, and they are going on a field trip to a local pumpkin patch. She showed pictures to the students of how the farmer plants the seeds, what they look like at each stage of their growth, and what nutrients the seed will need as they grow. She tells students they will have an opportunity to ask questions and allows students to think of some questions they might like to ask regarding the growth of the pumpkins. Mrs. Sandy then tells the students that they will get to go into the pumpkin patch and choose a pumpkin to take home for Halloween. She also asks the students to share examples of appropriate behavior and what to say to the farmer when they get their pumpkin.

Narrative advance organizers share information in a story format.

Mrs. Sandy's Kindergarten class is going on a field trip to a local pumpkin patch. She told them the following story:

"When I was about your age, we went to my Uncle Fred's farm one weekend during the fall. He told us he had something beautiful to show my family. We rode the hay wagon out to the field, and it was speckled with hundreds of orange balls. When we got down from the wagon, we ran to see what they were, and he told us they were pumpkins! He showed us the seeds he used to plant and told us

how they grew and what they would look like when they were ready to pick. And guess what? There were several just ready for us to take home! We loaded three pumpkins on the wagon and went back to the house. Aunt Sandy had just taken pumpkin pie out of the oven and it was ready to eat. Boy! Was it yummy!"

Appendix E: Sample Grade 1 Advance Organizers

Create advance organizers for new stories or new informational text and share with students prior to reading. Advance organizers can help to establish characters, settings, details, events, connections in information, and similarities and differences in texts that students are about to read or events in which students are going to participate. (RL.1.2, RL.1.3, RL.1.7, RL.1.9, RI.1.2, RI.1.3, RI.1.8, RI.1.9)

Use advance organizers like:

- KWL charts
- Flowcharts
- Outlines
- Webs—descriptive, concept
- SQRRR strategies
- 5W and How
- Alphaboxes

Use expository advance organizers to describe the new content to be learned. Here is an example:

Mrs. Harper's Grade 1 class is going on a field trip to the Wright Brothers National Museum to learn about how man learned to fly. She tells students they will listen to a park ranger who will talk to them about how the Wright Brothers built bicycles, experimented with gliders, and ended up creating a powered engine. She shares that students will go to the Flight Room to learn about how the brothers developed their first successful plane. Students will then go to the camp buildings to see how the Wrights lived and where they worked—especially a hangar where a replica of the 1903 flyer is stored. A visit to the Kite Building will allow students to watch demonstrations on how the Wrights tested the winds. Finally, students will walk out to the flight line to see the markers that show take-off points and chart the paths of their first flights.

A narrative advance organizer could look like this:

I remember one of the best vacations I ever had is when we visited the Wright Brothers National Monument near Kitty Hawk. My older sister worked there, and she was able to give us a special tour of the museum. We saw a couple of short films about how men tried to fly. They really had some crazy ideas! Then she took us to see replicas of the bicycles and gliders the Wrights created. We also got to see a cabin with furniture similar to what would have been available back then. The hangar had a replica of a 1903 flyer they built. The best part was touring the Kite Building. We learned about how the Wrights studied wind patterns using kites. Then we got to build kites of our own and flew them outside, just like the Wright brothers would have done.

To teach skimming, introduce the book *How People Learned to Fly* by Fran Hodgkins (2007) (EX). Students can skim the information to become familiar with the details in the book. You could create an outline. Supply the main headings and let students suggest the supporting details. Read the book aloud and complete the organizer as you read.

Appendix F: Sample Parent Letter

Date:

Dear Parent or Guardian:

This week we have worked on the following skills or concepts in class:

Please let your son or daughter share with you the above skills or concepts as he or she practices them at home. As you share this time with your child, it would be helpful if you would look for the following as your child practices:

Your child and I appreciate your time as you help him or her achieve success through practice.

Sincerely,

Appendix G: Products and Performances List

The following list of products and performances gives you suggestions for alternative homework assignments, projects, or performance assessments. You will find activities to address a wide range of grade levels and student abilities suitable for the implementation of CCSS.

ABC Books
Acrostic poems
Advertisements
Animated movies
Annotations
Anthology
Art gallery
Art product
Artifact analysis
Attribute chart
Audiotape
Autobiography
Banner
Bibliography
Biographical sketch
Blueprints
Board games
Book cover
Bookmark
Brochure
Bulletin board
Bumper stickers
Captions
Cartoons
CD covers
Ceramics
Characterizations
Character study
Chart
Children's story

Choral reading
Classroom decorating
Clay sculpture
Coat of arms
Codes
Collage
Collections
Comic strips
Commemorative stamps
Commercials
Comparisons
Computer programs
Computer quiz games
Costume creations
Creative writings
Crossword puzzles
Database
Demonstrations
Diagrams
Diary
Dictionary of terms
Diorama
Directions
Displays
Double-entry journal
Dramatic dialogue
Dramatic reading
Dramatizations
Drawings
E-mail projects

Editorials
Essays
Etching
Event
Experiment
Eyewitness report
Fable
Fairy tale
Family tree
Feature story
Fiction
Film
Film critique
Finger painting
Flags
Flannel board
Flip book
Floor plan
Flowchart
Foods
Formula
Forum on an issue
Game
Glossary
Graph
Greeting card
Haiku
Hidden pictures
Historical document
Historical fiction
Hypothesis telling
Hypothesis writing
I-search paper
Illuminated manuscript
Illustrated story
Illustrations
Infomercial
Interview
Invitation
Jewelry
Joke telling
Journals
Lab report
Labels
Learning center

Legal briefs
Letter of advice
Letter to the author
Letter to the editor
Letter — personal
Letter — persuasive
Lists
Literary critique
Literary letter
Logo
Logs (reading)
Lyrics
Magazine articles
Map
Machine
Mask
Matrix
Maze
Menus
Mind map
Mini-lesson
Mobile
Model
Module
Montage
Mosaic
Movie clip
Mural
Museum exhibit
Musical instrument
Myths
Needlework
New tool
News report
Newsletter
Newspaper articles
Note cards
Obituary
Observations
Oral defense
Oral presentations
Outline
Painting
Pamphlet
Panel discussion

Pantomime
Papier-mâché
Paraphrase
Parody
Pen-pal project
Photo album
Photo essay
Picture story
Plan
Play
Poetry
Poetry anthology
Political cartoon
Poll
Pop-up book
Portfolio
Position paper
Poster
Pottery
Presentation
Press conference
Project cube
Prototype
Puppet
Puppet show
Puzzle
Questionnaire
Q & A session
Quiz show
Radio program
Rap
Reaction paper
Readers theatre
Rebus story
Recipe
Recipe book
Recommendation
Report
Research paper
Response paper
Résumé
Riddle

Road map
Role-play
Satire
Schedule
Science fiction
Scrapbook
Script
Sculpture
Shoebox collection
Short story
Signs
Silk screen
Simulation
Skit
Slide show
Slogan
Song
Speech bubbles
Speeches
Spelling bee
Sports story
Spreadsheet
Stitchery
Storyboard
Story poem
Story map
Summary
Survey
Tables
Tall tale
Television program
Terrarium
Thematic unit
Time line
Transparencies
Tri-fold
Venn diagram
Videotape
Weather report
Written conversation
Worksheet

Appendix H: Verbs to Question

The verbs listed below can be found on many different lists and are generally broken down into separate categories. It may be more useful to categorize them into just two alphabetized lists. In the first list are verbs that are considered by most teachers to be lower-level recall verbs. The verbs in the second list are generally considered to be higher-order verbs.

LOWER-ORDER VERBS

add	interpret
ask	know
choose	label
classify	list
compare	listen
conclude	locate
contrast	match
convert	memorize
count	name
define	observe
demonstrate	omit
describe	outline
determine	paraphrase
differentiate	predict
discover	read
discuss	recall
display	recite
distinguish	recognize
estimate	record
explain	relate
express	repeat
extend	rephrase
find	report
generalize	restate
how	retell
identify	retrieve
illustrate	review
infer	rewrite

say	translate
select	underline
show	what
spell	when
state	where
summarize	which
tell	who
trace	why

HIGHER-ORDER VERBS

adapt	deduct
agree	defend
analyze	delete
apply	demonstrate
appraise	derive
argue	design
arrange	determine
assemble	develop
assess	diagnose
assume	diagram
award	differentiate
build	discover
calculate	discriminate
categorize	dispute
change	dissect
classify	distinguish
code	divide
combine	draw conclusions
compare	editorialize
compile	elaborate
compose	employ
compute	examine
conclude	execute
connect	experiment
construct	explain
contrast	explore
convince	formulate
create	hypothesize
criticize	illustrate
critique	imagine
debate	improve
deduce	infer

integrate
interpret
interview
invent
judge
justify
make up
manipulate
maximize
measure
minimize
model
modify
operate
order
organize
originate
paint
participate
perceive
perform
plan
practice
predict
prepare
pretend
prioritize
produce
propose
prove
rank
rate

rearrange
reason
recommend
reconstruct
record
relate
reorganize
revise
role-play
rule on
select
separate
sketch
solve
specify
state a rule
substitute
suggest
summarize
support
survey
teach
test
theorize
transfer
uncover
use
validate
value
verify
visualize
write

References

Anderson, V., & Hidi, S. (1988/1989). Teaching students to summarize. *Educational Leadership, 46,* 26–28.

Bransford, J., Brown, A., & Cocking, R. (1999). *How people learn: Brain, mind, experience, and school.* Washington, DC: National Academy Press.

Brookbank, D., Grover, S., Kullberg, K., & Strawser, C. (1999). Improving student achievement through organization of student learning. Chicago: Master's Action Research Project, Saint Xavier University and IRI/Skylight. (ERIC Document Reproduction Service No. ED 435094).

Cooper, H. (1989). Synthesis of research on homework. *Educational Leadership, 47*(3), 85–91.

Cooper, H., Lindsay, J. J., Nye, B., & Greathouse, S. (1998). Relationships among attitudes about homework, amount of homework assigned and completed, and student achievement. *Journal of Educational Psychology, 90*(1), 70–83.

Dale, E. (1969). *Audio-visual methods in teaching.* New York: Holt, Rinehart & Winston.

Davis, O. L., & Tinsley, D. (1967). Cognitive objectives revealed by classroom questions asked by social studies teachers and their pupils. *Peabody Journal of Education, 44,* 21–26.

Education Northwest. (2005*). Focus on effectiveness: Integrating technology into research-based strategies.* Retrieved from Northwest Educational Technology Consortium website: www.netc.org/focus/.

Fillipone, M. (1998). *Questioning at the elementary level.* Master's Thesis, Kean University. (ERIC Document Reproduction Service No. ED 417 431).

Fisher, D., & Frey, N. (2007). *Checking for understanding: Formative Assessment techniques for your classroom.* Alexandria, VA: Association for Supervision and Curriculum Development.

Fowler, T. W. (1975, March). An investigation of the teacher behavior of wait-time during an inquiry science lesson. Paper presented at the annual meeting of the National Association for Research in Science Teaching, Los Angeles. (ERIC Document Reproduction Service No. ED 108 872).

Johnson, D. W., & Johnson, R. T. (1999). *Learning together and alone: Cooperative, competitive, and individualistic learning.* Boston: Allyn and Bacon.

Jones, F. A. (1908). *Thomas Alva Edison: 60 years of an inventor's life.* New York: Thomas Y. Crowell & Company.

Kagan, S., & Kagan, M. (1997). *Kagan cooperative learning smart card.* San Clemente, CA: Kagan Publishing.

Kuhn, M. (2009, June 22). Generating and testing hypotheses is not just for science [McRel blog]. Retrieved from http://mcrel.typepad.com/mcrel_blog/2009/06/generating-and-testing-hypotheses-is-not-just-for-science.html?cid=6a010536aec25c970b0115724ac441970b.

Lavoie, D. R., & Good, R. (1998). The nature and use of prediction skills in biological computer simulation. *Journal of Research in Science Teaching, 25,* 334–60.

Lawson, A. E. (1998). A better way to teach biology. *The American Biology Teacher, 50,* 266–78.

Leach, S. (2010, February 2). Generating and testing hypotheses is not just for science [McRel blog]. Retrieved from http://mcrel.typepad.com/mcrel_blog/2009/06/generating-and-testing-hypotheses-is-not-just-for-science.html?cid=6a010536aec25c970b0115724ac441970b.

Lehrer, R., & Chazen, D. (1998). *Designing learning environments for developing understanding of geometry and space.* Mahwah, NJ: Erlbaum.

Markman, A. B., & Gentner, D. (1996). Commonalities and differences in similarity Comparisons. *Memory and Cognition, 24*(2), 235–49.

Marzano, R. J., Pickering, D. J., & Pollock, J. (2001). *Classroom instruction that works: Research-based strategies for increasing student achievement.* Alexandria, VA: Association for Supervision and Curriculum Development.

Meyer, B. F., & Freedle, R. O. (1984). Effects of discourse type on recall. *American Education Research Journal, 21,* 121–44.

National Council of Teachers of Mathematics. (2000). Principles and standards for school mathematics. Reston, VA: Author.

National Governors Association Center for Best Practices, Council of Chief School Officers. (2010). Common core state standards for language arts. Washington, DC: Author.

Redfield, D. L., & Rousseau, E. W. (1981). A meta-analysis of experimental research on teacher questioning behavior. *Review of Educational Research, 51*(2), 237–45.

Vatterott, C. (2009). *Rethinking homework: Best practices that support diverse needs.* Alexandria, VA: Association for Supervision and Curriculum Development.

White, B. Y., & Frederickson, J. R. (1998). Inquiry, modeling, and metacognition: Making science accessible to all students. *Cognition and Instruction, 16*(1): 3–117.

About the Author

Michelle Manville taught elementary and middle school for sixteen years in Missouri and served as the curriculum coordinator for her district for ten years. She also served on many local and state curriculum committees and was a Missouri Select Teacher as Regional Resource curriculum trainer for two years.